Introduction

Rivers have been at the centre of Scottish life for thousands of years. the earliest settlers a river meant – a source of food, drinking water, transport. Over the centuries, villages, towns and all of Scotland's cities have grown and developed along the banks of a river.

From the Industrial Revolution, when Scotland was one of the manufacturing powerhouses of Europe, until the long decline of heavy industry in the 20th century, rivers were integral to Scotland's economic development.

As towns and cities attempt to reinvent themselves in the wake of that decline, rivers and riverbanks are crucial to regeneration, providing key destinations for residential developments, offices, leisure and recreation. Water activities such as rowing, sailing, kayaking, canyoning and fishing are increasingly popular, and wildlife is making a comeback as the environment begins to recover from pollution.

From source to sea, a river passes through a variety of landscapes – from mountains to hills, towns to cities, countryside to concrete – and the best way to discover the scenery, wildlife, architecture and history is to walk.

The increasing number of paths and walkways along riverbanks present plenty of opportunities to explore. Whatever your ability – walking at high or low level, tackling tough terrain or a

The River Spey is a restless river, one filled with salmon and sea trout, bounded by vast tracts of woodland, backed by several of Britain's highest mountains and surrounded by a huge range of wildlife. Its voyage results in an ever-changing landscape as each year the river, swollen with snowmelt, unleashes a massive volume of water, which carves new channels and islands, generating its own perpetually evolving course.

Lonely little Loch Spey, which sits above Loch Laggan in Lochaber, beneath the big rounded Monadhliath, marks the beginning of the River Spey and its wild and wonderful 107-mile journey.

Scotland's fastest and second longest river quickly descends beside General Wade's historic road and beneath Garva Bridge, the oldest bridge spanning the Spey. Once through Spey Dam, it enters Badenoch & Strathspey and a landscape dominated by the immense Cairngorm Plateau, where peaks such as Braeriach and Cairn Gorm dwarf everything in sight.

The hills reduce in size as the River Spey enters Moray, renowned the world over as whisky country. Against this more understated backdrop, the river twists and turns towards the coast, eventually spilling into the North Sea at Spey Bay, between Lossiemouth and Buckie.

4   River Spey from Creagan an Fhithich

With a catchment of more than 3000 square kilometres, the River Spey passes mountains, great tracts of woodland, including the Caledonian pinewoods of Rothiemurchus, Abernethy and Glenmore, lonely lochs and flatter plains as journey's end is approached. Early tributaries include the Markie Burn, the River Mashie and the River Truim, with the Feshie, the Druidh and the Nethy joining later on.

Throughout its passage, the River Spey is a rural river which encounters no cities. Instead a selection of attractive settlements, including Kingussie, Aviemore, Grantown-on-Spey, Fochabers, Elgin and Portgordon, sit on or a few miles from its banks, with many fine walks radiating from them.

For the hillwalker, there are plenty of choices along all but the final stages of the river's journey. Big peaks on the fringes of the Spey catchment, such as A' Mharconaich and Braeriach, take several hours to summit, whilst lower hills like Craigellachie, Meall a' Bhuachaille and Ben Rinnes take less effort but still offer good walking and far-reaching views.

The 25 routes in this guide have been chosen to illustrate the diversity of walking to be found on or near the banks of the River Spey as it travels from source to sea. Many of these routes are circular to take in the best of the scenery in the area that surrounds each stage of the river's journey. The walks also highlight the wildlife, architecture and history to be found along the way. Deer, otter, golden eagle, osprey, ptarmigan, mountain hare, snow bunting, dotterel, wagtail, curlew, arctic tern, red-breasted merganser and goldeneye are just some of the wildlife that this landscape sustains, whilst buildings such as Ruthven Barracks, Elgin Cathedral and Loch an Eilein Castle are not only visually striking, they also have fascinating and often turbulent histories.

Early history

It has taken a long time for the River Spey to find its path – four ice ages, or several hundred million years, to be a little more precise. Over this almost unimaginable timescale, the river system has slowly weathered and moulded its course over a bed of schists, gneiss, granite and sandstone – and this amalgamation of rock types makes the River Spey one of the cleanest in Scotland. As it hits the wide alluvial plain of Strathspey the riverbed loosens, with the Spey pushing soil and sediment along. When Spey Bay is approached, the river begins to pick up speed, dragging enormous amounts of shingle with it, which alter its shape and route.

The derivation of the name Spey is unclear. It appeared on Ptolemy's map of Scotland as *Tvesis* in 150AD, but it took another 1300 years before it was referred to as the River Spey. One suggestion as to its meaning is 'Vomit' or 'Gush', from the pre-Celtic word *squeas*. Certainly, the speed at which the River Spey travels means this may be a more apt label than it would first appear.

Its clean, fast-flowing waters would have made the River Spey an appealing means of transport for the earliest Stone Age and Neolithic settlers who began to utilise its environs (although not the Cairngorm Plateau) some 6000 years ago. Salmon and trout, game birds and berries and nuts from the surrounding woodland would have provided a rich source of food.

Like much of Scotland, the Bronze and Iron Ages saw people lay down more definite roots and by the time the Romans marched northwards around the 1st century AD, several small settlements existed. The Romans had little success in establishing themselves in the North East of Scotland, with the Cairngorm forming an almost impenetrable barrier, although it is thought that the battle of Mons Graupius in 83/84AD, which saw a superior Roman army defeat the Caledonians, could have been fought near Elgin.

It was The Picts who were most successful in settling in the region, particularly in the great Caledonian pinewoods of Rothiemurchus and Abernethy. Along with the Gaels, they were the dominant race in the North East and formed a redoubtable force against the Roman advance (it was the Romans who purportedly named the Picts, meaning 'the Painted People', alluding to

the face paint the Picts sometimes wore).

Many of the hill and place names along the River Spey reflect the languages of the Picts and Gaels. *Aber* translates from Pictish as 'Mouth of the River', and so Aberlour and Abernethy have their roots in the Pictish language, whilst Gaelic can be seen in names such as Braeriach, Meall a' Bhuachaille, Craigellachie and Buckie.

From the time of the very first settlers, fish have been something of a lifeline for many of those who have lived near the banks of the Spey. During prehistoric times, salmon were fished at the mouth of the Spey and it is the jewel in the crown of Scotland's great salmon rivers – it is also acknowledged as the premier sea trout river in the country. Hugely popular with anglers, fishing on the River Spey is vital economically to many of the communities along its length.

The river also led to the creation of the Spey Cast. It is different from the normal fly cast, as it is double handed. When developed during the 19th century, it prevented anglers from catching the woodland overhead along narrower sections of the river. Traditional overhead casting couldn't avoid this and the Spey Cast is now used worldwide.

Other industries such as shipbuilding and timber exports were already big business (as was cattle thieving, which had been prevalent along the Spey since the 14th century), although these are now consigned to the past.

It wasn't until the 18th and 19th centuries, with the building of many bridges across the Spey (prior to this it was mainly forded or crossed by ferry), General Wade's road network and the arrival of the railway, that towns and villages such as Kingussie, Aviemore and Grantown-on-Spey developed around various water-driven mill industries that utilised the power of the Spey.

Today, it is the outdoor industry that draws people to the river and its environs – walking, cycling, skiing, canoeing, white-water rafting and wildlife watching are just a few of the recreational pursuits enjoyed on or near the Spey.

After spending the day outdoors, a dram is the obvious way to relax and whisky has become synonymous with the Spey, pumping millions of pounds into the economy annually, with Moray as its spiritual home.

Originally hailed for its medicinal qualities, whisky is now one of Scotland's major exports and is fundamental to the survival of the towns and villages along much of the River Spey, particularly in Moray. The mild climate, pure spring water and abundant supplies of fragrant golden barley provide the ideal ingredients for the 'water of life'. The Spey supports over half of all whisky distilleries in Scotland, including Glenfarclas, Cardhu, Aberlour and Craigellachie, as well as Glenfiddich and Glenlivet, the two biggest selling whiskies in the world.

How to use this guide

The 25 walks in this guidebook run geographically from the River Spey's source at Loch Spey in the Monadhliath to Spey Bay where it empties into the North Sea. Wherever possible, the start/finish for each walk is easily accessible by public transport and, if not, there is car parking nearby. Many of the walks are also easily reached from villages and towns along the length of the river, with access to shops, places to eat, accommodation and public toilets.

Each route begins with an introduction detailing the terrain walked, the start/end point (and grid reference), the distance covered, the average time to walk the route and the relevant Ordnance Survey (OS) map.

Public transport information is also detailed, although this may change from time to time and should be checked before commencing any of the walks in this guide (travelinescotland.com).

A sketch map shows the main topographical details of the area and the route. The map is intended only to give the reader an idea of the terrain, and should not be followed for navigation – the relevant OS map should be used for this purpose.

Every route has an estimated round-trip time. This is for rough guidance only and should help in planning, especially when daylight hours are limited. In winter, or after heavy rain, extra time should be added to allow for difficult conditions underfoot.

Risks and how to avoid them

Some of the routes in this guidebook are challenging hillwalks while others cross remote terrain. The weather in Scotland can change suddenly, reducing visibility to only a few metres. Winter walking brings distinct challenges, particularly the limited daylight hours and low temperatures which, over higher ground, can fall well below freezing. Please take this into consideration before commencing any of the hillwalks in this guide. Preparation should begin well before you set out, and your choice of route should reflect your fitness, the conditions underfoot and the regional weather forecasts.

None of the hillwalks in this guide should be attempted without the relevant OS map or equivalent at 1:50,000 (or 1:25,000) and a compass.

Even in summer, warm waterproof clothing is advisable, and footwear that is comfortable and supportive with good grips is a must. Don't underestimate how much food and water you need, and remember to take any medication required, including reserves in case of illness or delay. Do not rely on receiving a mobile phone signal when out walking in the hills and remote areas. It is a good idea to leave a route description with a friend or relative in case of emergency.

There is a route for almost all levels of fitness in this guide, but it is important to know your limitations. Even for an experienced walker, colds, aches and pains can turn an easy walk into an ordeal.

Those routes that venture into the hills or rough terrain assume some knowledge of navigation with use of map and compass, though these skills are not difficult to learn. Use of Global Positioning System (GPS) is becoming more common; however, while GPS can help pinpoint your location on the map in zero visibility, it cannot tell you where to go next and, like a mobile phone, should not be relied upon.

A few walks in this guide cross hill or mountain terrain and in winter it is recommended that you take an ice axe and crampons – and know how to use them – on these. Such skills will improve confidence and the ease with which such a route can be completed. They will also help you to avoid or escape potentially dangerous areas if you lose your way. The Mountaineering Council of Scotland provides training and information (mcofs.org.uk). However, for most of the routes in this guide, proficiency in walking and navigation is sufficient.

Access

Until the Land Reform (Scotland) Act was introduced in 2003, the 'right to roam' in Scotland was a result of continued negotiation between government bodies, interest groups and landowners. In many respects, the Act simply reinforces the strong tradition of public access to the countryside of Scotland for recreational purposes. However, a key difference is that under the Act the right of access depends on whether it is exercised responsibly.

Landowners also have an obligation not to unreasonably prevent or deter those seeking access. The responsibilities of the public and land managers are set out in the Scottish Outdoor Access Code (outdooraccess-scotland.com).

The walks within this guidebook cross land that is only fully accessible due to the co-operation of landowners, local councils and residents. Some of the routes pass through farms, golf courses and streets, and near homes and gardens.

Cyclists and horse riders often use the paths and tracks, and anglers and canoeists may use the river and riverbanks. Consideration for others should be taken into account at all times and the Scottish Outdoor Access Code must be followed.

At certain times of the year special restrictions are implemented at low level and on the hills, and these should be respected. These often concern farming, shooting and forest activities: if you are in any doubt, ask. Signs are usually posted at popular access points with details: there should be no presumption of a right of access to all places at all times.

The right of access does not extend to the use of motor vehicles on private or estate roads.

Seasonal Restrictions
Red and Sika Deer Stalking:
Stags: 1 July to 20 October
Hinds: 21 October to 15 February

Deer may also be culled at other times for welfare reasons. The seasons for Fallow and Roe deer (less common) are also longer. Many estates provide advance notice of shoots on their websites.

Grouse Shooting:
12 August to 10 December

Forestry:
Felling: All Year
Planting: November to May

Heather Burning:
September to April

Lambing:
March to May – although dogs should be kept on leads at all times near livestock.

The Cairngorms from near Newtonmore

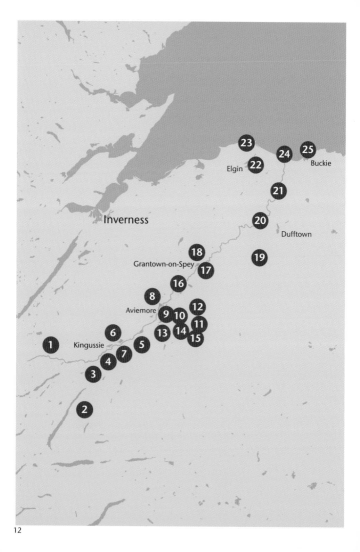

Inverness

Grantown-on-Spey

Aviemore

Kingussie

Elgin

Dufftown

Buckie

The Walks

Garva Bridge to Melgarve

Distance 12.75km/8 miles
Time 3 hours
Start/Finish Car park at Garva Bridge
GR NN522947
Terrain Narrow glen road
Maps OS Landranger 34 and 35
Public transport No public transport
to start. Garva Bridge is 9.5km from
Laggan along a single-track road

When it was built by General Wade in
1731, the 40km-long Military Road,
which crosses the Corrieyairack Pass
to link the villages of Fort Augustus
on Loch Ness with Laggan on the
banks of the Spey, was the highest
road in Britain. The tarred 6km
section from Garva Bridge to
Melgarve Bothy offers a simple but
historic approach to the pass along a
picturesque section of the Spey's
early meanderings. Strong walkers
might be tempted to continue over
rough, pathless ground to reach the
source of the river at Loch Spey.

► The walk begins from a small car park
at Garva Bridge, reached by following
the minor road for almost 10km west
from Laggan. Cross the bridge – another
example of General Wade's handiwork –
and head northwest along a narrow
stretch of road as it climbs gradually into
more remote mountain country.

Rainbow near Melgarve

▶ The road soon levels off, bounded on each side by craggy peaks, and makes its way past a stand of pine woodland, with the views beginning to extend west along the glen towards the Corrieyairack Forest. Once past the woodland, the road drops down to run alongside the Spey once again which, even at this early stage, is already quite a significant river, its waters flowing quietly through the empty landscape.

▶ As Melgarve comes into view, look out for Alltachorain, a lonely cottage that sits on a bend of a watercourse – one of the Spey's major early tributaries – from which it takes its name. There is a standing stone nearby.

▶ Just before Melgarve, the road crosses a bridge and narrows to a track. Follow this for a short distance to reach Melgarve Bothy, a good spot for spying deer. For walkers wishing to complete the journey towards the source of the River Spey, bear left at the bothy and follow a track past a cottage to a bridge over the Allt Yairack, just before it enters the Spey. The route continues southwestwards from here.

▶ Once you are ready to return to civilisation, simply retrace your steps to Garva Bridge, enjoying the scenery and wildlife throughout.

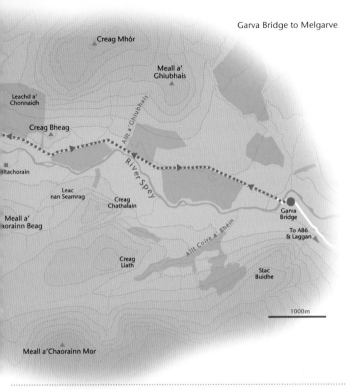

Walking through History Crossing the Monadhliath Mountains, and offering the most direct route from Speyside to the Great Glen, the Corrieyairack Pass has been well-used down the centuries – not least by drovers heading to the great cattle trysts at Crieff and Falkirk. In 1731, General George Wade was given the task of constructing a military road through the pass as a supply route for troops and goods between Fort Augustus and Ruthven Barracks – part of the government's wider effort to gain control of the Highlands. Some 500 troops were employed to construct the road and the many bridges along its length, and it remains the longest surviving stretch of General Wade's road in Britain. Today, it is on the route of a rather different but equally controversial feat of engineering – a major power transmission line upgrade that runs for 220km between Beauly, north of Inverness, and Denny, near Stirling.

Garva Bridge

A' Mharconaich

Geal-charn, Beinn Udlamain and A' Mharconaich

Distance 17.25km/10.75 miles
Time 7 hours 30
Start/Finish Car park at Balsporran Cottages GR NN628792
Terrain Mountain paths, with some sections where paths are indistinct. Several steep ascents and descents
Map OS Landranger 42
Public transport Scottish Citylink Service M91 Car from Edinburgh and Inverness to Balsporran Cottages on the A9, 6.5km south of Dalwhinnie

The sprawling mountains of Geal-charn and A' Mharconaich rise high above the Drumochter Pass at the southern edge of the Cairngorm National Park. Combining these two Munros with the outlying Beinn Udlamain (also a Munro) makes for a big day in the hills with nearly 1100m of ascent, but the panoramic views and sheer sense of space are ample reward. Sections of the walk are featureless with indistinct paths, so good navigation skills are required in poor weather.

► From the car park just off the A9, follow the road past Balsporran Cottages and cross the railway line with care to join a track that runs to the right of the Allt Coire Fhar. Ignore a path branching right and continue to a wooden bridge, bearing right onto a grassy path a little after this to begin the steep – and sometimes soggy – climb through the heather. Height is gained quickly, with fine views opening out to the rolling hills on the eastern side of the Drumochter Pass.

► The path soon veers southwest to gain a flatter crest where a steady climb over stony ground takes you to the domed summit of Geal-charn. At 917m, it is a Munro – but only just!

► Just beyond the summit, an obvious path descends southwest, then south into the wilder and lonelier reaches of these mountains. Look for red deer crossing the broad plateau and, if you're really lucky, you might also catch sight of a golden eagle working the thermals above.

► Descend to a bealach above Coire Fhar, bearing right onto another path. At this point keep an eye out for an indistinct path on the left that ascends steeply SSE onto a featureless plateau a little south of the summit of A' Mharconaich. The border between Perth & Kinross and Inverness-shire splits the high ground in two here, while it also forms the very southern tip of the Cairngorm National Park.

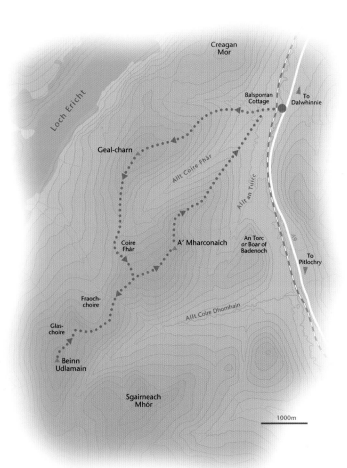

► Head right and make your way southwest along the broad ridge towards Beinn Udlamain. Much of the terrain here is lacking in any features, but a line of old fenceposts marking the regional boundary provides some guidance.

► A gentle climb above Fraoch-choire leads to a short, steep pull to the stony summit of Beinn Udlamain – at 1011m, the highest point of the walk. Again, the summit makes a great vantage point, with a particularly impressive outlook across Loch Ericht to mighty Ben Alder, one of Scotland's finest mountains.

Horsing Around The unusual name A' Mharconaich (pronounced 'a varkaneech') has an equally curious translation from Gaelic as 'The Place of the Horse'. It is an historic name associated with a time when horses, rather than sheep or deer, called the high moorland and mountaintops home (horses must have once been a common sight in the Drumochter hills as there is another mountain of the same name just north of Dalwhinnie). To the south, A' Mharconaich overlooks a great tract of land known as Dalnaspidal Forest, although it is a forest in name only. As with elsewhere in the Highlands, this is a deer forest – a sporting estate that has been historically managed for deer rather than trees.

► Retrace your steps along the ridge to pick up a good path above Coire Fhar, climbing gradually northeast to reach A' Mharconaich, the final summit of the route with arguably the best view.

► From the summit, bear left to descend north above the steep eastern face of A' Mharconaich. The path soon swings right to descend steeply northeast along a ridge. The descent is far more dramatic than many would give these mountains credit for, and is one of the very best sections of the walk.

► However, as the floor of the glen is reached, the path becomes muddy, overgrown and indistinct in places, so it's a matter of picking your way along to return to the Allt Coire Fhar. Choose a crossing point – your feet might get a little wet – and turn right onto the outbound track to return to the car park at Balsporran.

Loch Ericht from Geal-charn

The Falls of Truim

Falls of Truim

Distance 10km/6.25 miles
Time 3 hours
Start/Finish Falls of Truim Car Park
GR NN681922
Terrain Field, riverbank and
woodland paths, single-track road
Map OS Landranger 35
Public transport No public transport
to start

This walk visits the dramatic Falls of
Truim before climbing to the Truim
Woods Viewpoint – with wonderful
views along the early reaches of the
River Spey. Good paths and tracks
line the walk, although dogs must
be kept on leads when crossing
farmland at Crubenbeg.

► Start at the Falls of Truim car park,
just off the A9 on the minor road
heading south towards Dalwhinnie via
Crubenmore. Backtrack on foot from
here to reach a little road for
Crubenbeg. Once on this, look for a
gate on the right giving access to a path
signposted for the Falls of Truim. This
leads through birch woodland, with the
falls soon visible through the trees.

► After viewing the falls, climb back up
to the gate and turn right to follow the
road over General Wade's bridge.
Immediately after the bridge, turn right
through a gate (signposted Riverside
Circular) to accompany a tree-lined path
high above the River Truim, with great
views of the gorge below. At a
waymarker, turn left to head away from
the river and continue to a junction.
Turn right here and, at the next
waymarker, fork left. Beyond a gate,
cross a field on an indistinct path, then
turn right onto a wide farm track.

► Follow this track past a house
and, once through a gate, immediately
bear left onto an indistinct path,
continuing over a track to reach a ruined
stone building. Turn left through a gate
(at a green waymarker) where the path
now climbs an embankment to reach a
farm track to the right of a house at
Crubenbeg.

Fantastic Falls The River Truim rises high in the hills above Drumochter, dropping
some 450m to reach the River Spey at Invertruim. It is a journey that has seen the
water cut a deep cleft through the granite bedrock to create the spectacular Falls of
Truim, just south of Newtonmore. Here, a series of waterfalls cascade beneath an
old stone bridge – one of many built by General George Wade and his army as
part of an effort to wrestle control of the Highlands following the 1715 Jacobite
uprising. Mosses, liverworts, ferns and lichens all prosper within the damp micro-
climate of the gorge, while the Truim itself is well-regarded for its salmon fishing.

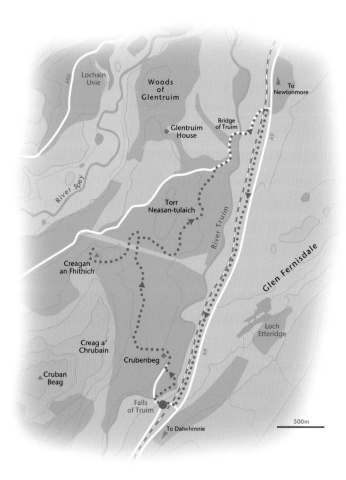

► Turn right to follow the track uphill. At the top, turn left at a waymarker onto a path which veers along the left-hand edge of the field, eventually climbing to a gap in the fence. After passing through the gap, turn right onto the signposted 'Old Right of Way for the Perth Road'. This grassy track leads you alongside a stone dyke, with far-reaching views across Speyside.

► As the route drops gradually towards Glen Truim Woods, the rocky slopes of Cruban Mor and Cruban Beag rise sharply to your left. The wall is soon left behind, with a fence now keeping you company as you walk downhill to a gate.

► Once through the gate, continue along the track, ignoring a branch to the right for Glen Truim Woods. At the next signed junction, take the track on the left signposted for the Truim Woods Viewpoint. This climbs – steeply in places – to reach a vantage point on the summit of Creagan an Fhithich, complete with a cairn and bench.

► Once you've enjoyed the views over Badenoch and towards the Cairngorm, retrace your steps down to the junction with the main track. Turn right onto the outbound route, then left around a barrier to follow a wide forestry track into Glen Truim Woods.

► This drops gently to reach a fork: keep left and continue to a stile by a gate. Cross this to reach a single-track road and turn right, following the road past a small cottage at the entrance to Glentruim House.

► After another cottage, the road crosses the old stone Bridge of Truim and then climbs steeply towards the A9. Once across a railway bridge, turn right onto a cycle/walkway (the old A9) and continue south. Although sandwiched between the railway line and the busy main road, the route is sheltered by woodland and a grass embankment, and is surprisingly quiet.

► Continue along this for 3km to return to the Crubenmore/ Dalwhinnie road. Turn right, cross the railway line and return to the car park.

Speyside from Creagan an Fhithich

The Cairngorm from the Wildcat Trail

Wildcat Trail, Newtonmore

Distance 10.5km/6.5 miles
Time 3 hours
Start/Finish Newtonmore Railway
Station GR NN716984
Terrain Countryside, field, riverbank
and woodland paths, single-track
road. The route is waymarked
Map OS Landranger 35
Public transport Regular Scotrail
Services from Glasgow, Edinburgh
and Inverness to Newtonmore.
Regular Scottish Citylink Service
M91 from Edinburgh and Inverness
to Newtonmore

**The Cairngorm are usually
associated with long, gruelling
mountain days, but there are also
plenty of lower-level walks, of which
the Wildcat Trail is a particularly
good example. Following excellent
paths and tracks that encircle the
village of Newtonmore, this tranquil
route offers local history, plenty of
wildlife, plus views of those big
Cairngorm mountains.**

► From Newtonmore Railway Station,
head along Station Road for a short
distance before turning left along the
side wall of the last building in a row of
railway cottages. Pass through a gate
and take the left branch at a fork to
continue through two more gates and
reach a level crossing.

► Cross the railway line with care and,
after another gate, bear left and walk
along a narrow path to cross a
footbridge. Follow the edge of a field to
the banks of the River Spey, turning
right to accompany the river upstream
on a gentle meander through beautiful
countryside.

► Hugging the north bank of the river,
the route passes beneath first an iron
railway bridge and then a roadbridge,
where the River Calder joins the Spey.
Continue along the right-hand bank of
the Calder until the path climbs up to
the road over the Calder Bridge at the
western edge of Newtonmore.

A Dark History Newtonmore owes much of its existence to the Highland
Clearances – a dark chapter in Scottish history that saw thousands of crofting
families 'cleared' from the land, largely to make way for more profitable sheep
grazing. Many settled along the banks of the Spey where there was room to grow
crops. The expansion of Newtonmore continued with the building of a new
parliamentary road by Thomas Telford in 1817, which linked nearby Kingussie with
Fort William, and the re-routing of the main road north from Perth to Inverness
through the village. Visitors came in even greater numbers with the arrival of the
railway in 1863, and the town remains a popular tourist destination today.

▶ Cross the road (A86) with care and turn left through a gate to follow a path, going through another gate and then passing Banchor Cemetery. The narrow path now climbs steeply, passing through two more gates to gain a viewpoint with stunning views to the Cairngorm massif.

▶ From the viewpoint, turn sharp left and continue through woodland above the tumbling River Calder, eventually reaching a gate. Once through this, the path can be boggy as it rises quite steeply to reach a picturesque bend in the river with views across the water to the hills of Creag nan Abhag and An Torr. Continue to the tarmac Glen Road, turning right to follow the single-track road down through a gate beside a cattle grid.

▶ Just after a cottage, turn left onto another narrow road which climbs gently past several more properties. After the last cottage, the path splits: head left through a gate onto a boggy farm track, which crosses a field and then forks. Go right to enter old birch woodland, passing a cairn. Ignore a path on the right for Newtonmore and instead continue straight on, passing through several gates, to reach a minor road (there is an optional diversion to visit a Pictish stone circle).

▶ Head straight across the road and cross a footbridge, then turn left. After crossing another bridge, take a left, then a right at a waymark to join a narrow path that passes through Strone, once a thriving crofting township.

Wild at Heart The Wildcat Trail is named after the last remaining large mammal predator in Britain. Considerably bigger than a domestic cat, with a distinctive blunt, ringed tail, the Scottish wildcat is a fierce and elusive animal. In recent centuries, hunting, habitat destruction and persecution have led to a dramatic decline in numbers. Today, one of the biggest issues is hybridisation with domestic cats, leading some conservationists to believe that there could be fewer than 100 pure Scottish wildcats left in the wild. Much easier to spot are the many colourful and lifesize wildcat models tucked away in gardens, on windowsills, up trees, on phoneboxes and in all manner of crafty places around Newtonmore. They have been hidden by villagers as part of the Wildcat Experience – a fun outdoor activity for families, with certificates and prizes available, depending on how many are spotted. For more details, visit the Wildcat Centre on Newtonmore Main Street, where an illustrated booklet and map of the Wildcat Trail is also available.

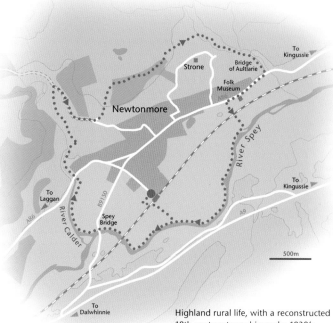

Highland rural life, with a reconstructed 18th-century township and a 1930's working farm.

► Beyond a gate, a good path descends alongside the fast-flowing Allt na Feithe Buidhe, eventually crossing the river via a footbridge. Cross a stile into woodland, and continue to eventually gain the A86. Turn right onto a grassy path above the road, passing through two gates to join a pavement that leads past the Highland Folk Museum. This excellent living history museum (admission is free) provides an evocative portrayal of

► Just past the entrance to the museum, turn left down a narrow road, crossing a bridge over the railway line to reach a gate. From here, a path follows the edge of Newtonmore Golf Course before sweeping right to skirt along the Spey once more. Continue beside the river, eventually crossing two stiles to reach the outbound path. Turn right and retrace your steps to the railway station.

The Wildcat Trail above the River Calder

Uath Lochans

Distance 3.5km/2.25 miles
Time 1 hour
Start/Finish Uath Lochans Car Park
GR NN835022
Terrain Woodland paths and tracks
following waymarks with some
steep ascents
Map OS Landranger 35
Public transport Regular Scottish
Citylink Service M91 from
Edinburgh and Inverness to
Kincraig. This leaves around 4.5km
to the start

A cluster of four small lochs set deep
in the heart of Inshriach Forest in
Glen Feshie, Uath Lochans are a
haven for waterbirds, dragonflies
and other wildlife. This simple but
scenic loop passes the lochs
before climbing Creag Far-leitire,
with fine views over the forest.

► Walk through the car park to a
green/red/white marker post and turn
left onto a broad forestry track that runs
to the right of the lochans. Follow the
track, passing a path to the right (the
return route), as it continues beneath
the wooded slopes of Creag Far-leitire.

► The route soon begins to climb
gradually, following green/red
waymarks, with the gradient increasing
as the track twists and turns up the
hillside to a path on the right. Take this

path and continue to climb, the incline
easing a little as views across the Uath
Lochans open up. Keep to the right
edge of the crag (the drops here are
near vertical, so take care) as the route
meanders ever upwards with fine views
over Speyside.

► Continue past a bench and
viewpoint to reach a clearing at the top
of the crag where there is another
bench next to a boulder. This is a good
spot to pause and enjoy the views.

► From here, the path turns left and
descends, steeply at first, back into
woodland to meet a junction. Turn right
here and again at the next junction
where the path continues through the
woods to connect with the Badenoch
Way (a 17.5km walking route from
Dalraddy to near Kingussie, which
mostly follows the River Spey).

► This leads down to another junction
where you again turn right to head
gently downhill with good views to the
north. At the next red waymark, where
the Badenoch Way peels away to the left,
instead continue straight on to the next
fork. Bear right here, with the vertical
slopes of Creag Far-leitire coming back
into view. The track skirts the base of the
crag, eventually returning to the
outbound route. Turn left and walk the
last 100m or so back to the start.

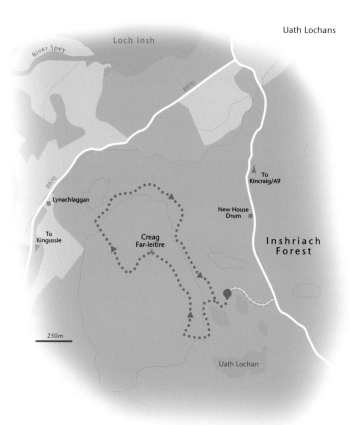

Loch Insh

Uath Lochans

River Spey

B970

To Kincraig/A9

Lynachlaggan

New House Drum

To Kingussie

Creag Far-leitire

Inshriach Forest

250m

Uath Lochan

Ice Land Creag Far-leitire climbs to more than 335m in height and was formed during the last ice age, when the surrounding landscape was gouged by the enormous pressure of a glacier. The imprint left by massive chunks of ice also formed the Uath Lochans. The crag makes an excellent vantage point for looking north along the River Spey and southwards over the forested moorland of Glen Feshie and the rolling prospect of the high mountains above it. Much of Glen Feshie is a Site of Special Scientific Interest due to its river landforms.

Uath Lochans from Creag Far-leitire

Speyside from Creag Bheag

Creag Bheag and Kingussie

Distance 5.5km/3.5 miles
Time 2 hours
Start/Finish Kingussie Railway
Station GR NN757004
Terrain Pavement, minor road,
woodland and hillside paths
Map OS Landranger 35
Public transport Regular Scotrail
Services from Glasgow, Edinburgh
and Inverness to Kingussie. Scottish
Citylink Service M91 from Edinburgh
to Inverness and Aviemore

**Rugged Creag Bheag stands
sentinel-like over the town of
Kingussie, with far-reaching views
across Badenoch and Strathspey
from its summit. With fine woodland
covering its lower slopes and well-
maintained paths to the summit, it
makes for a great all-round
exploration of the town's environs.**

► From Kingussie Railway Station, turn
left and follow Station Road (B970) to
where it joins Newtonmore Road (A86)
in the town centre. Turn right along this
and left onto Gynack Road before shortly
turning left again to walk through
Ardvonie Car Park.

► At the car park's right-hand corner
(by some public toilets), join a path that
climbs above an area of grassland to
reach Tait's Brae, opposite West Terrace.
Turn right and follow Tait's Brae
(signposted Creag Bheag West Terrace
Circular) past several houses.

► As the road swings right at Middle
Terrace, bear left and follow a rough
track to a gate on your left. Go through
this to join a wide track that begins a
gradual climb through attractive
woodland. Depending on the season,

Gordon's Town Kingussie grew as a planned village from the early 19th century
under the guidance of the fourth Duke of Gordon, the then owner of Kingussie Estate.
Prior to this, a smaller settlement existed on the south side of the Spey at Ruthven.
There had been a castle here since the 13th century, built on the mound now
occupied by the ruins of Ruthven Barracks – a government garrison that was burnt
down by retreating Jacobites following the Battle of Culloden in 1746. Like many
Highland settlements, the arrival of the railway in 1863 changed Kingussie's fortunes,
transforming it from a tiny hamlet to a prosperous town and fashionable holiday
resort. With the excellent Wildcat Trail, the Highland Folk Museum, Ruthven Barracks
and the nearby Highland Wildlife Park, Kingussie remains a popular destination for
visitors and an excellent base for exploring the wider area. It's also a great place to
catch a game of shinty – the governing body for the sport was founded here and
Kingussie's team has enjoyed huge success down the years.

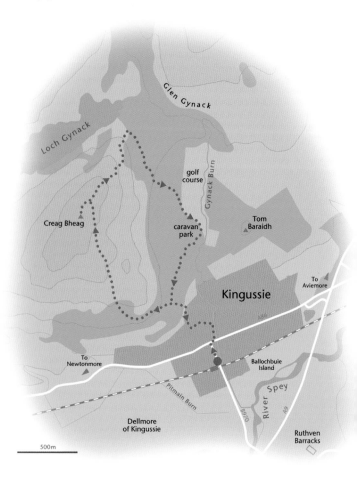

it's worth keeping your eyes and ears sharpened for a glimpse of a roe deer or the rat-a-tat-tat of a woodpecker.

► It can be boggy at first, but the path improves as it climbs to a fork. Bear left and stick to the main path which, after a steep pull, exits the woodland through a gate. Continue straight on, climbing to the left of an old wall over the heather-clad slopes of Creag Bheag.

► Although steep in places, the path improves as it climbs and makes for some great walking. The gradient eases as the rugged ridge of Creag Bheag is gained at a cairn. Turn left and head along a narrow, undulating path to reach the summit.

► Once rested, retrace your steps along the well-defined path to the cairn beside the outbound route. Instead of descending, keep to the high ground, heading northeast along the bumpy crest, passing more cairns to reach a stone shelter at the end of the ridge. From here, a well-maintained path leads downhill, steeply at times, towards woodland with an unexpected view opening out across Loch Gynack.

► Continue to walk downhill to meet a waymarked junction just above the loch and turn right onto a path, signposted Kingussie Golf Course Circular, which heads through birch woodland. There are some short, boggy sections to negotiate as the path swings to the right, but it soon improves as it passes through a clearing.

► The path makes the gradual descent through lichen-encrusted oak and birch woodland, eventually passing through a gap in a wall, after which it bears left through a gate. Continue for another few metres, then turn right and follow a trail that drops gently through a firebreak in the trees, with Kingussie Golf Course running to the left. A firmer path then heads down to a gate beside a caravan park.

► Instead of going through the gate, turn right and take a path which follows the fenceline back into woodland where it meets a junction. Turn left and drop back down to the outbound track, which exits the woodland at Middle Terrace. Retrace your steps into Kingussie.

Kingussie from Creag Bheag

Gynack Burn

Ruthven Barracks and the Gynack Burn

Distance 6km/3.75 miles
Time 1 hour 45
Start/Finish Kingussie Railway Station GR NN757004
Terrain Pavement, minor road, woodland paths
Map OS Landranger 35
Public transport Regular Scotrail Services from Glasgow, Edinburgh and Inverness to Kingussie. Regular Scottish Citylink Service M91 from Edinburgh and Inverness to Aviemore

Kingussie owes its expansion as a town to the Gynack Burn which once powered several mills as it flowed from Loch Gynack to the River Spey. The town's roots, however, can be traced to a site on the south side of the river by Ruthven Barracks. This walk visits both.

▶ From Kingussie Railway Station, turn right onto Ruthven Road (B970) and head south, with the Gynack Burn running parallel to the road on your left. After a while, the road crosses the Spey and then ducks under the A9, before climbing gradually and then swinging left to reach a car park by the imposing ruins of Ruthven Barracks. Turn left through a gate and climb a path to explore the barracks – an eerie experience, especially if here alone.

▶ Retrace your steps along Ruthven Road, continuing past the railway station and the Gynack Memorial Gardens to reach Newtonmore Road (A86) in the town centre. Turn right, then left onto Gynack Road (signposted Gynack Mill Circular) and walk past Ardvonie Car Park, following the road as it climbs to the left of the Gynack Burn.

▶ Look out for a flight of steps on the right and go down these and the path beyond to cross a bridge over the burn. To the right is the rear entrance to one of the mills, now a hotel and restaurant. Continue straight on along the path, climbing through birch woodland to the right of the burn to reach a viewpoint overlooking the remains of a dam built in the 1800s.

▶ The path now continues steeply, swinging right to a junction. Turn left here, then left again at a fork to climb ever higher above the gorge, the path enveloped by native woodland. The route soon bears right away from the burn to a fenced section of path between some houses.

▶ Beyond a gate, turn left onto a road and, after 50m or so, turn left again to go down some steps and cross back over the water – a lovely stretch of the burn

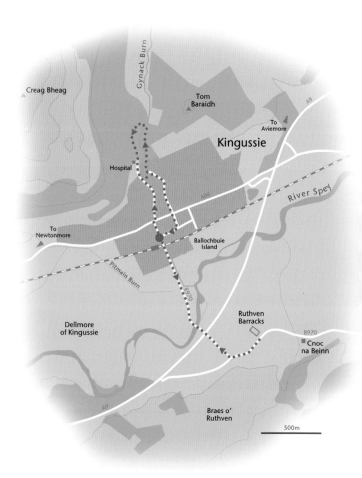

Creag Bheag

Gynack Burn

Tom Baraidh

To Aviemore

A9

Kingussie

Hospital

A86

River Spey

To Newtonmore

Ballochbuie Island

Pitmain Burn

B970

Dellmore of Kingussie

Ruthven Barracks

8970

Cnoc na Beinn

A9

Braes o' Ruthven

500m

with several waterfalls. Carry on along the path and then turn left to follow Gynack Road downhill past the entrance for St Vincent's Hospital, which began life in the early 1900s as the Grampian Sanatorium for patients with tuberculosis. Eventually this brings you to the outbound path above the bridge crossed earlier in the walk.

► Turn left to go down the steps and back over the bridge, this time bearing right on the other side to climb a steep flight of steps to a gate. Head through this and walk along handsome Boa Vista Road to a junction. Turn right here onto Ardbroilach Road, which drops downhill towards the town centre, passing an impressive clocktower.

► Continue straight over the High Street (A86) to join King Street and walk as far as the junction with Spey Street. Turn right here to cross the Gynack Burn one last time before turning left onto Station Road and returning to the railway station.

Defensive Capability The atmospheric location of Ruthven Barracks, marooned on a mound whenever the nearby Insh Marshes are flooded by the River Spey, is a sight worth viewing in itself. But this spot also has a long and turbulent history. Originally the site of a 13th-century castle built by the powerful Comyn clan, it was later home to the Stewarts of Badenoch – most notably the infamous Wolf of Badenoch. After the 1715 Jacobite uprising, the site was chosen as the location for one of a series of fortified barracks that the government attempted to tighten its grip on the Highlands. All remains of the earlier castle were removed in the construction of Ruthven Barracks which were designed to house around 120 troops, plus a stable block. Having survived an attempted capture by around 200 Jacobites in August 1745 – when a force of just 12 Redcoats managed to resist the attack – the garrison surrendered to a much larger force a few months later. It was also here that several thousand Jacobites, in retreat following defeat at Culloden in 1746, received a message from Bonnie Prince Charlie that they should flee and save themselves. Before dispersing, the Jacobites set fire to the barracks, leaving the site pretty much as it can be seen today.

Ruthven Barracks

Craigellachie Birch Pool

Craigellachie

Distance 5.25km/3.25 miles
Time 2 hours
Start/Finish Aviemore Railway
Station GR NN896123
Terrain Pavement, minor road,
woodland and hillside paths. Steep
ascent onto Craigellachie
Map OS Landranger 36
Public transport Regular Scotrail
Services from Glasgow, Edinburgh
and Inverness to Aviemore. Regular
Scottish Citylink Service G10 from
Glasgow and Inverness and Service
M91 from Edinburgh and Inverness
to Aviemore

Rugged Craigellachie looms over
Aviemore, its lower slopes cloaked in
birch woodland. This walk climbs
through the wildlife-rich woods that
make up much of this National
Nature Reserve, visiting two lochans
before gaining a rocky summit with
views over Rothiemurchus Forest to
the Cairngorm Plateau beyond.

▶ From Aviemore Railway Station, turn
left and walk south along Grampian
Road (the main B9152 through town).
Not long after leaving the bustle of the
town centre behind, look for a right turn
onto a road signposted for the youth
hostel, catholic church and nature
reserve. Follow this road as it climbs past
the hostel and church to join a broad
woodland path. Continue to a fork,

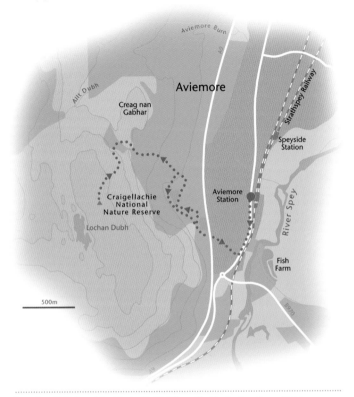

Standing Tall 'Stand Fast Craig Elachie' (from the Gaelic *Seas Buan, Creag Eileachaidh*) is the battlecry of Clan Grant whose Strathspey seat was once Castle Grant near Grantown-on-Spey. The cry refers to Craigellachie, and a burning beacon on its summit was used to rally the Grants to arms – the clan crest contains an image of a burning hill. It is easy to understand why the Grants used Craigellachie as a meeting point as the panorama is far-reaching and includes much of Badenoch and Strathspey, the big, lonely Monadhliath and a number of the renowned Cairngorm peaks, including Meall a' Bhuachaille, Cairn Gorm and Cairn Toul.

where you go left through an underpass beneath the A9 into Craigellachie National Nature Reserve.

► From here, the path rises gently through lovely birch woodland. At a fork, head right and walk to Loch Puladdern, the first of two lochans hidden amongst the trees. Bear left to walk around the left edge of the lochan and then alongside a burn. At a junction, turn right to continue beneath the wooded slopes of Craigellachie. When you meet a path on the left, take this as far as a waymarker, now going right onto a narrow path that climbs gently to the second lochan.

► At the next waymarker, bear right, cross a burn by stepping stones and skirt the east shore of the lochan. Once away from the loch, you come to a wider, stony path. Turn left and climb steadily, with the steep crags of Craigellachie visible high above. Ignore a path on the left (which is used on the return) and continue to climb as the path zigzags steeply beneath the crags.

► The path then veers left and climbs a flight of steps to gain a viewpoint which looks out over Aviemore. With the neighbouring hillsides swathed in woodland, it's a slice of Scotland as it once was. An excellent path continues south, passing a small cairn to reach a larger summit cairn with extensive views to Rothiemurchus Forest and the Cairngorm Plateau beyond.

► Retrace your steps to the path you passed on the way up. Turn right here and follow the narrow trail southwest, traversing the lower slopes of Craigellachie just above the second lochan visited earlier.

► At a junction, turn right and drop down to reach a second junction near Loch Puladdern. Bear right here and walk back down to the outbound path, bearing right again to retrace your steps beneath the A9 and into Aviemore. Once at Grampian Road, turn left and return to the train station.

The Monadhliath from Craigellachie

Scots pine, Rothiemurchus

Rothiemurchus

Distance 7.25km/4.5 miles
Time 1 hour 30
Start/Finish Coylumbridge
GR NN915107
Terrain Woodland paths and tracks
Map OS Landranger 36
Public transport Regular Scotrail Services from Glasgow, Edinburgh and Inverness to Aviemore. Regular Scottish Citylink Service G10 from Glasgow and Inverness and Service M91 from Edinburgh and Inverness to Aviemore. Stagecoach Service 31 from Aviemore to Coylumbridge

The network of paths that criss-cross Rothiemurchus makes for delightful walking in one of the largest areas of remnant Caledonian pinewood in Scotland. Tread quietly on this straightforward stroll through the forest and you may spot red squirrel, Scottish crossbill, crested tit and some of the other charismatic wildlife that makes its home here.

► The walk begins from a lay-by on the B970 at Coylumbridge, beside the entrance to the Rothiemurchus Camp and Caravan Park. From here, follow a broad track that runs to the right of the camping ground.

► The track passes through two gates and heads through atmospheric woodland, reaching a fork after a few hundred metres. Bear left here, following signage for the Lairig Ghru (right is for Glen Einich) to continue through a scattering of trees where the fast-flowing Am Beanaidh can be heard to the left.

► The track soon enters an area of more dense woodland before crossing a footbridge and passing through a gate. Continue south along the track, negotiating two more gates and a further footbridge.

► At a junction a short distance beyond the second gate, turn sharp right (signposted for Loch an Eilein) onto a path that runs west over heather moorland, with great views to the Lairig Ghru as well as the giants of Braeriach and Sgor Gaoith. The path eventually passes lovely Lochan Deo ('Sparkling Loch') before reaching a crossroads.

► Turn right for Coylumbridge here and walk north to pass through two gates, with the woodland gradually thinning as progress is made. The path eventually descends through more woodland, going through another gate by a cattle grid and then past a cottage.

► After 250m or so, go straight ahead to join the outbound track and retrace your steps alongside the camping ground to Coylumbridge.

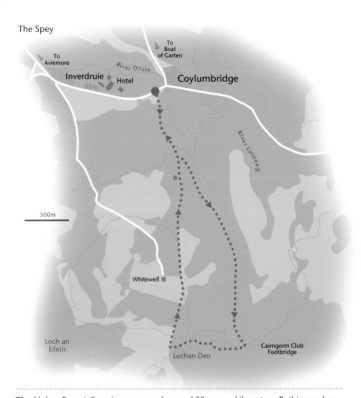

The Spey

To Boat of Garten

To Aviemore

River Druie

Inverdruie

Hotel

Coylumbridge

B970

River Luineag

500m

Whitewell

Loch an Eilein

Lochan Deo

Cairngorm Club Footbridge

The Living Forest Covering an area of around 30 square kilometres, Rothiemurchus Forest is believed to contain more than 10 million trees, the majority of which are gnarled old Scots pines. Starting in neighbouring Abernethy, this chunk of ancient forest runs south through Rothiemurchus Estate to Glen Feshie, making it the largest area of remnant Caledonian pinewood in Scotland. Stretching from the banks of the Spey to the summit of Braeriach almost 1300m up on the Cairngorm Plateau, the estate has been in the care of the Grants of Rothiemurchus for several centuries. Their conservation-minded approach has focused on regeneration of the pinewoods, a specialist habitat that is home to a celebrated rollcall of wildlife, including red squirrel, pine marten, crested tit, Scottish crossbill and capercaillie. The wildlife here is vulnerable to disturbance, and in some cases extremely rare, so please keep dogs under close control.

Rothiemurchus woodland

Loch Morlich

Distance 6km/3.75 miles
Time 1 hour 30
Start/Finish Loch Morlich Car Park
(charge) GR NN958097
Terrain Woodland and lochside paths
and tracks
Map OS Landranger 36
Public transport Regular Scotrail
Services from Glasgow, Edinburgh
and Inverness to Aviemore. Regular
Scottish Citylink Service G10 from
Glasgow and Inverness and Service
M91 from Edinburgh and Inverness
to Aviemore. Stagecoach Service 31
from Aviemore to Loch Morlich

Cradled within the beautiful
Glenmore Forest, a circuit of the
shores of Loch Morlich is hard to
beat. The route offers no real
navigation issues, while the
predominantly flat paths, and a
seasonal beach café to incentivise
tiring parties early on in the outing,
make this a good choice for families.

► The walk begins from the car park at
the northwestern edge of Loch Morlich.
Before starting, take a moment to enjoy
the view across the loch to the Northern
Corries and beyond. Home to the
Cairngorm Mountain Ski Centre, snow
can linger in these corries and on the
ridges well into the summer months.

► Cross the main road to join a wide
forestry track (signposted for Glenmore
Forest Park) and immediately turn right
onto a woodland path, known as the
Old Logging Way. Follow this path east
for around 1.5km to a junction just
before the driveway to Cairngorm Lodge
Youth Hostel, opposite Glenmore Shop.

► Turn right to backtrack along the
roadside verge for just 40m, before
turning left into a car park signposted
for Loch Morlich Watersports. Continue
straight on through the car park onto a
woodland path, going left at a fork and
passing some public toilets.

The Big Glen Combining high mountains, swathes of ancient forest and even a
sandy beach at Loch Morlich, Glenmore Forest Park has much to offer. Acquired by
Forestry Commission Scotland in the 1920s – and becoming its second forest park
in 1948 – in more recent times much has been done to encourage regeneration of
native species within the park. Non-native conifers have been removed, allowing
birch, aspen, juniper, rowan and, of course, Scots pine, to prosper, with the
ultimate aim of encouraging an even greater diversity of wildlife. Such diversity
extends out onto the open hill where a herd of reindeer – reintroduced by a
Swedish reindeer herder in the 1950s – roam freely. For details on how to visit the
herd, ask at the Cairngorm Reindeer Centre.

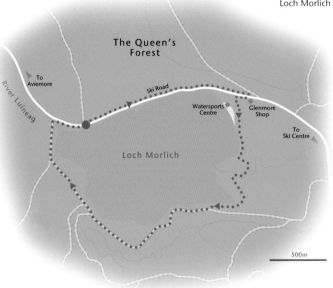

The Queen's Forest

River Luineag

To Aviemore

Ski Road

Watersports Centre

Glenmore Shop

To Ski Centre

Loch Morlich

500m

► Continue past the sandy beach at the northeastern end of Loch Morlich, cross a footbridge over a burn, then walk through mixed woodland to reach a junction beside the fast-flowing Abhainn Ruigh-eunachan, close to where it flows into Loch Morlich. Turn left here to reach a bridge over the river.

► After crossing this, turn right along the riverbank. At a fork, head left to meander through birch and larch woodland, bearing left again at a fork to reach a junction. Turn right here and right again when you encounter another fork. The well-maintained soon returns to the shore of the loch.

► At the next junction, turn right onto a broad forestry track, which continues above the loch, eventually forking right. A bridge then crosses a burn, after which the track narrows to a path and runs along Loch Morlich's western shore, terminating at the Rothiemurchus Lodge estate road.

► Turn right and follow the estate road, eventually crossing a bridge over the River Luineag. Just before the main road, turn right and then bear right again onto a woodland path which returns to Loch Morlich car park.

Loch Morlich at dawn

Creag nan Gall, Glen More

An Lochan Uaine and the Thieves' Road

Distance 5.25km/3.25 miles
Time 1 hour 30
Start/Finish Glenmore Visitor Centre
Car Park (charge) GR NN976099
Terrain Woodland paths and tracks
with a couple of steep ascents
Map OS Landranger 36
Public transport Regular Scotrail
Services from Glasgow, Edinburgh
and Inverness to Aviemore. Regular
Scottish Citylink Service G10 from
Glasgow and Inverness and Service
M91 from Edinburgh and Inverness
to Aviemore. Stagecoach Service 31
from Aviemore to Glenmore

This route follows woodland paths
and tracks, including a stage of the
historic Thieves' Road, to the
magical green waters of An Lochan Uaine.
The return journey traverses the
lower, wooded slopes of Meall a'
Bhuachaille, offering extensive views
across the Cairngorm National Park.

► From the Glenmore Visitor Centre
car park, follow the track to the right of
the visitor centre. This takes you around
a barrier and across a lane to pass the
Reindeer Centre, joining the single-track
road just beyond. After about 50m,
bear left onto a cycleway which
continues beside the road to pass
Glenmore Lodge, Scotland's National
Outdoor Training Centre.

► A forest track now takes over from the
single-track road, with the cycleway
curving down to join it just after the gate
marking the road end. Known as the
Thieves' Road, this peaceful route (signed
for Forest Lodge and Nethy Bridge),
bears northeast through typically
atmospheric Caledonian pinewood.

► Continue as the track travels above
the Allt na Feith Duibhe, the steep
slopes of Meall a' Bhuachaille rising
beyond. It is easy going for much of the

Bandit Country The quiet, unobtrusive Rathad nam Meirleach (the Thieves' or
Caterans' Road) once ran all the way from Lochaber to the fertile pastures of
Moray. It was used by groups of Highlanders who supplemented their income by
stealing cattle from more prosperous glens to guide back to their own lands –
action that, unsurprisingly, led to running battles as the rightful owners of the
cattle tried to recover their livestock. In later years, the Thieves' Road was used by
drovers driving their herds through Rothiemurchus and on to the Lairig an Laoigh
('the Pass of the Calves') on the way to the great livestock trysts at Falkirk, Perth,
the Scottish Borders and North England.

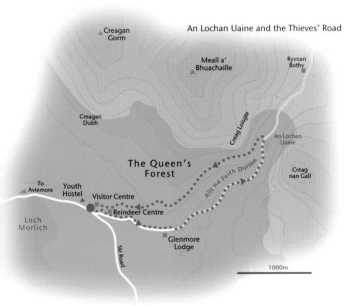

way and An Lochan Uaine ('The Little Green Loch') is soon reached – the shore is accessed down a flight of steps. The colour of the loch – enchanting if you catch it in the right light – is usually attributed to minerals found in the underlying rock, but the less scientific explanation has it that fairies who once lived here washed their garments in the water. Whatever you believe, it's a joy to linger here.

▶ Return up the steps and go straight across the outbound trail onto a blue waymarked path. This takes you down a flight of steps and across a boardwalk before climbing steeply up more steps onto Meall a' Bhuachaille's lower slopes.

▶ The steep ascent makes for rapid height gain, with majestic views to Cairn Gorm and the striking Northern Corries of Coire an Sneachda and Coire an Lochain. The gradient eventually eases as the path, which can be a little rough underfoot, continues in a southwesterly direction high above the glen.

▶ At a clearing, continue straight on along a forest track which makes a gradual descent into The Queen's Forest, eventually reaching a single-track road by a house. Turn left onto this road and head down past another house to reach the Reindeer Centre. Go right to take the path back to Glenmore Visitor Centre.

An Lochan Uaine

Creagan Gorm

Ryvoan Bothy

Meall a' Bhuachaille and Creagan Gorm

Distance **9.5km/6 miles**
Time **5 hours**
Start/Finish **Glenmore Visitor Centre Car Park (charge) GR NN976099**
Terrain **Woodland and hillside paths and tracks. Some steep ascents and descents**
Map **OS Landranger 36**
Public transport **Regular Scotrail Services from Glasgow, Edinburgh and Inverness to Aviemore. Regular Scottish Citylink Service G10 from Glasgow and Inverness and Service M91 from Edinburgh and Inverness to Aviemore. Stagecoach Service 31 from Aviemore to Glenmore**

Reached via fine paths, the rounded slopes of Meall a' Bhuachaille rise high above Glenmore Forest Park, with sweeping views across the Cairngorm National Park. Throw in a diversion to the neighbouring peak of Creagan Gorm and a descent that passes Ryvoan Bothy and this is a great introduction to some of the bigger hills in the area.

► The walk begins from the Glenmore Visitor Centre car park, near the eastern edge of Loch Morlich. Cross a bridge at the left-hand corner of the car park and follow a road as it climbs to the upper car park. Once around a barrier, turn right to cross another bridge and then go left onto a stony track signposted for Meall a' Bhuachaille. This immediately begins to climb steeply through Glenmore Forest, giving the legs and lungs a warm-up for what lies ahead.

► The incline eases as a junction is reached. Turn left here to join a fine path that climbs gradually, before bearing right at a fork. The path heads above the treeline onto open hillside, with the heather-clad slopes of Meall a' Bhuachaille rising ahead. During the summer, look out for dotterel, golden plover and skylark, as well as enjoying magnificent views across Loch Morlich and the great forest of Rothiemurchus.

► The excellent path now bears right and climbs to a col between Meall a' Bhuachaille and Creagan Gorm. To climb Creagan Gorm, head left here and descend west at first before making the steady ascent to the summit. It's a fine vantage point but, if anything, there is even better to come.

► Retrace your steps to the col, this time continuing east to zigzag steeply up a stony path to gain the 810m summit of Meall a' Bhuachaille, its flatter top marked with a stone shelter.

► After soaking up the views, look for the path bearing left from the summit shelter as it begins to drop gradually across a grassy hillside, initially in a northeasterly direction. At a fork, bear right to descend eastwards, with several sections of steps making the steeper parts a bit less rough on the knees.

► There are wonderful views of the little green teardrop of An Lochan Uaine, with the steep descent eventually easing for a final stroll to Ryvoan Bothy.

► Turn right to join the broad Thieves' Road, which drops southwest into Glen More – its name derives from the cattle thieves who once drove livestock this way. At a junction bear right to pass the waters of An Lochan Uaine. Although there are several offshoot paths, stick to the main track for another 1.25km before branching right onto a cycleway just before a barrier at the start of a single-track road.

► This runs parallel to the road, passing Glenmore Lodge. Once the cycleway rejoins the road, just carry on along the verge. Soon, when the road swings left to join the main Ski Road, go straight on along the track in front of the Reindeer Centre and cross a lane to pass round the barrier directly opposite. The track continues beyond to take you back to the visitor centre and the start.

Shepherd's Peak Meall a' Bhuachaille, which means 'Hill of the Herdsman' in Gaelic, is the highest point of the Kincardine Hills, a range that rises to the north of the much bigger Cairngorm. Its name reflects the use of the area by shepherds from the numerous small farms that were once scattered around the hill, who would drive their animals onto the fertile slopes to graze during the summer. Standing slightly apart from the main peaks of the Cairngorm, the views from the summit of Meall a' Bhuachaille extend northeast along the softer landscape of Speyside to Ben Rinnes, southeast to the big rough tops of Bynack Beg and Bynack More and, on a clear day, all the way northwest to the Moray Firth and the vast bulk of Ben Wyvis in Easter Ross.

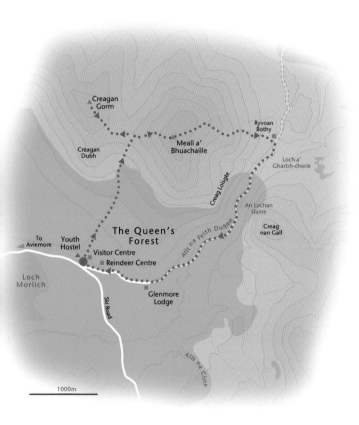

Creagan Gorm

Ryvoan Bothy

Creagan Dubh

Meall a' Bhuachaille

Loch a' Gharbh-choire

Creag Loisgte

An Lochan Uaine

Creag nan Gall

To Aviemore

Youth Hostel

The Queen's Forest

Visitor Centre

Reindeer Centre

Allt na Feith Duibhe

Loch Morlich

Ski Road

Glenmore Lodge

Allt na Ciste

1000m

79

Loch Morlich from Meall a' Bhuachaille

Loch an Eilein Castle

Loch an Eilein

Distance 6.5km/4 miles
Time 1 hour 30
Start/Finish Loch an Eilein Car Park
(charge) GR NN896086
Terrain Lochside and woodland
paths and tracks
Map OS Landranger 36
Public transport Regular Scotrail
Services from Glasgow, Edinburgh
and Inverness to Aviemore. Regular
Scottish Citylink Service G10 from
Glasgow and Inverness and Service
M91 from Edinburgh and Inverness
to Aviemore. Stagecoach Service 31
from Aviemore to Inverdruie. This
leaves just over 3km to the start

**Hidden within Rothiemurchus
Forest, Loch an Eilein and its island
castle ruins are among the most
photographed destinations in the
Cairngorm, yet little disturbs the
tranquillity here. An excellent path
loops around the loch, although the
trail around neighbouring Loch
Gamhna is not as well maintained
and can be boggy.**

► From the car park, make your way
along the woodland path to reach the
visitor centre. At a junction, head left
away from the centre and then bear
right to follow the shore of Loch an
Eilein. At an elevation of 250m, both
Loch an Eilein and nearby Loch
Gamhna are often frozen over during
the winter.

► Once across a footbridge that spans
the outflow of the loch, turn right onto a
broad estate track and carry on through
pine woodland, soon passing the red-
roofed Forest Cottage.

► As you meander through the
woodland, travelling clockwise around
the loch, there are tantalising glimpses
of both the water and the hills all around.
It's a peaceful setting, with the silence
most likely to be broken by the
scrambling of a red squirrel (look for
well-gnawed pine cones on the forest
floor) or the calls of classic pinewood
species such as the Scottish crossbill or
crested tit in the trees.

Limestone and Logging Looking carefully at the outflow of Loch an Eilein ('Loch of
the Island'), traces of a dam are visible – evidence of a semi-industrial past. In the
18th and 19th centuries, the water levels of the loch were raised to float logs
downstream to the Spey where they were processed. The abundance of limestone
outcrops nearby, plus timber for fuel, also saw the building of several limekilns
around the loch, with the remains of one close to the visitor centre. Limestone was
burnt in the kilns to provide a valuable powder that was used both in the building
trade and for improving agricultural land.

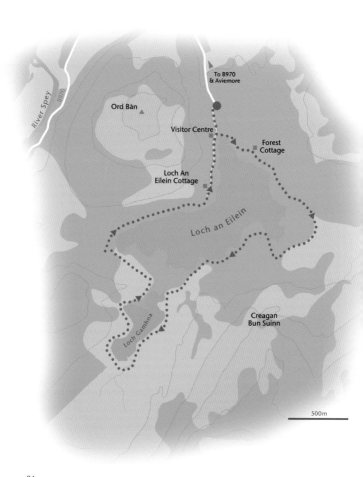

► After a while, the track crosses a footbridge before coming to a fork. Bear right here to pass through a gate (the left-hand path leads to the Lairig Ghru, Scotland's best-known mountain pass) and continue around the loch.

► Eventually the path crosses another footbridge before swinging right. Take the next path on the left to travel south around the much smaller Loch Gamhna. Boggy in places, the path passes beneath the steep slopes of Creag Dhubh before coming to a fork. Bear right here to eventually regain the Loch an Eilein path.

► Turn left and continue the easy stroll alongside Loch an Eilein, the pinewoods stretching as far as the eye can see. Just after a bench, turn sharp right at a junction (signposted 'Path') and walk along a broad woodland track above the shore.

► Once through a gate and past a lovely cottage, the route passes Loch an Eilein Castle, sitting just a short distance out in the water with its crumbling walls covered in undergrowth. Continue alongside the loch to return to the visitor centre, with the car park just beyond.

Island Home In all probability the island which gives Loch an Eilein its name is natural. It is thought that there has been some sort of defensive fortification on the island since the 13th century when the Bishop of Moray constructed a hall house surrounded by a defensive wall. During this time, Strathspey came under the jurisdiction of the Diocese of Moray and the island would have provided a secluded refuge for the Bishop. The first actual castle on the island seems to have been built in the 1380s when the notorious Wolf of Badenoch (Alexander Stewart, Robert the Bruce's great-grandson) constructed a towerhouse on the north end of the island. Some 10m high with 1.8m-thick walls which were surrounded by water, the castle would have held a formidable defensive position. Later extensions were added from 1600 by Patrick Grant of Rothiemurchus. The castle has seen several notable skirmishes down the years, not least when it was besieged by defeated Jacobites following the Battle of Cromdale in 1690, while its walls were also used to shelter Jacobite fugitives following Culloden more than half a century later.

Loch an Eilein

Ben Macdui from Braeriach

Snow on Braeriach

Braeriach

Distance 25km/15.5 miles
Time 8 hours
Start/Finish Loch Morlich (charge)
GR NN958097
Terrain Woodland and mountain
paths, with some sections where
paths are indistinct. Several steep
ascents and descents
Map OS Landranger 36
Public transport Regular Scotrail
Services from Glasgow, Edinburgh
and Inverness to Aviemore. Regular
Scottish Citylink Service G10 from
Glasgow and Inverness and Service
M91 from Edinburgh and Inverness
to Aviemore. Stagecoach Service 31
from Aviemore to Loch Morlich

A long and tough but memorable
route that climbs from the shores of
Loch Morlich to the summit plateau
of Braeriach – the third highest peak
in the British Isles and arguably the
finest mountain in the Cairngorm
National Park. The approach follows
excellent trails through pinewoods
to the famed Lairig Ghru, although
some later sections require care and
good navigation skills, particularly in
poor visibility.

► From the car park at the northwest
edge of Loch Morlich, follow the red
waymarkers west to the road. Turn left
as if heading back to Aviemore, then left
again to cross a bridge over the River

Luineag and into the Rothiemurchus
Estate. With Loch Morlich on your left,
head along the estate road, continuing
straight on at a signpost for the Lairig
Ghru – the famous mountain pass
through the Cairngorm.

► The estate road passes the waters of
Lochan nan Geadas and continues
southwest through picturesque
woodland to a fork after around 1km.

► Take the right branch, again
signposted for the Lairig Ghru, following
a path through more woodland to a
crossroads after another 1.25km. Turn
left here and follow the excellent path
southeast as it climbs gradually above
the Allt Druidh.

► As height is gained, the woodland
begins to thin until the path emerges
onto open hillside with great views
north along Speyside and south to the
mighty cliffs of Creag an Leth-choin
(better known as Lurcher's Crag, a
popular climbing spot). The deep
northern corries of Braeriach are also
now visible, peaking above Sron na
Lairige. In summer, the transition from
pinewood to heather moorland brings
with it a marked difference in wildlife to
look out for, with various species of
dragonfly and butterfly, as well as birds
such as skylark and meadow pipit, much
in evidence.

► After a while, the path drops down to the early reaches of the Allt Druidh. Once past a path peeling left to the Chalamain Gap (which heads to Glenmore on the east side of Loch Morlich), find a point to cross the river – be prepared for slightly wet feet! Continue along the west bank on the Lairig Ghru.

► After another 50m or so, turn sharp right to leave the Lairig Ghru for a recently-laid path that zigzags onto the shoulder of Sron na Lairige. This gives a steep, prolonged ascent as it picks its way south over a stony landscape with a couple of small boulderfields slowing progress a little.

► A wide, stony track then leads onto a more defined ridge where there are far-reaching views across the Lairig Ghru to the vertiginous cliffs of Lurcher's Crag and Cairn Lochan. The track narrows, with a good path continuing south, skirting the featureless summit plateau of Sron na Lairige.

► Stick to the main path as it descends to a col before a final steep pull onto the vast summit plateau of Braeriach. Take real care as the path runs close to the plunging cliffs of Coire Bhrochain, which are often corniced with deep snow well into the summer months.

► From the summit, retrace your steps down over Sron na Lairige, briefly along the Lairig Ghru and back through Rothiemurchus Forest to Loch Morlich, enjoying fine views throughout.

Passing Through In recent years, the Rothiemurchus Estate (which stretches to the summit of Braeriach) has done a huge amount of path improvement work, not just on Sron na Lairige, but also along the Lairig Ghru – arguably the most famous mountain pass in Scotland. For centuries, this high pass – rising to almost 900m in places – was an ideal through-route for cattle thieves, although it was later used primarily by drovers to drive their cattle between Aviemore and Braemar, a distance of more than 40km. Such was the importance of the pass for droving (and, therefore, the economy of the area) that men were sent up every spring to clear the paths of boulders left after the usually severe winter weather. Today, the pass is well-used by walkers, as well as participants in the annual Lairig Ghru Hill Race – with the current record for running the 43km between Braemar and Aviemore police stations standing at a little over three hours.

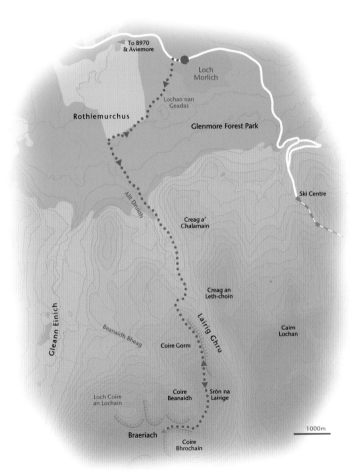

Creag an Leth-choin and the Lairig Ghru

Cairn Gorm

Cairn Gorm and Cairn Lochan

Distance 10.25km/6.5 miles
Time 5 hours
Start/Finish Coire Cas Car Park
GR NN990060
Terrain Mountain and moorland
paths with steep ascents. Some parts
of the Cairngorm Plateau are
featureless and run close to the
cliff edge
Map OS Landranger 36
Public transport Regular Scotrail
services from Glasgow, Edinburgh
and Inverness to Aviemore.
Scottish Citylink Service G10
from Glasgow and Inverness and
Service M91 from Edinburgh and
Inverness to Aviemore. Stagecoach
Service 31 from Aviemore to
Coire Cas

Although at a lofty 1245m, Cairn
Gorm is the sixth highest mountain
in Britain, this walk starts halfway up
its broad flanks, allowing a relatively
simple ascent. Once on the plateau
between Cairn Gorm and Cairn
Lochan, however, things change.
The route crosses a largely
featureless alpine-arctic landscape
on indistinct paths that hug the
edge of the Northern Corries, so
great care and good navigation
skills are essential – particularly in
poor visibility. The reward, on a
clear day, is one of the finest walks
in the Cairngorms.

► From the Coire Cas car park
(donations for path upkeep welcome),
climb the steps signposted 'Central
Staircase'. Turn right and follow a path
past the main buildings of the
Cairngorm Mountain Ski Centre, then
bear left at a fork. From here, climb
towards the funicular railway to
another path on the left, signposted
'Windy Ridge'.

► Join this excellent path and ascend
in a southeasterly direction onto the
lower slopes of Sron an Aonaich.
Already there are fine views back across
Loch Morlich and wider Speyside.
The climb is steep, but much of it is on
steps, making the going a lot easier.
Once on the broad ridge of Sron an
Aonaich, the gradient eases as the
path then continues south towards
Cairn Gorm, with the buttresses and
scoured flanks of Coire an t-Sneachda
coming into view.

► Eventually, the route passes to
the left of the Ptarmigan Restaurant –
the ski centre's top station – where a
left turn gains a stepped, roped path
that climbs steadily towards the domed
summit of Cairn Gorm. The roped
path ends close to the top, with a
rockier trail then continuing alongside
marker cairns to reach the summit
cairn and observation mast.

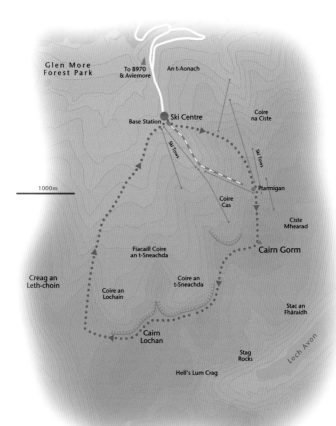

► From the summit, head in a southwesterly direction to pick up a path that descends gradually before contouring close to the edge of Coire an t-Sneachda. Great care is needed both here and later when skirting the edge of Coire an Lochain (together known as the Northern Corries – a hugely popular winter climbing destination).

► At a fork, keep left as the path begins to climb steadily past a cairn over a rounded, unnamed summit. The path then becomes less distinct as it descends west over rocky ground, although there are marker cairns to aid progress. At a col above Coire Domhain, a clearer path climbs steeply towards Cairn Lochan, although again take great care as the path runs close to the cliff edge.

► As the summit of Cairn Lochan is approached, the path swings sharp left at a craggy ridge and then climbs southwest over the featureless summit plateau with the complex corries of Cairn Toul catching the eye in the distance.

► Marker cairns aid progress (the summit itself is hard to make out), although they should not be relied upon. From the summit plateau, continue on a westerly bearing and then descend grassy slopes to reach the obvious path for Ben Macdui.

► Turn right here to follow a well-maintained path on a long, gradual descent – with views into the Northern Corries – all the way back to the ski tows and the Coire Cas car park.

Climbing Heaven The Northern Corries – Coire an t-Sneachda and Coire an Lochain – have long been a popular spot for winter climbing, combining ease of access, generally reliable conditions and a range of routes suitable for all standards. The cliffs are comprised of Cairngorm granite, a weathered rock that offers plenty of flakes, cracks and other features. Of the two, Coire an t-Sneachda has more to offer low- to mid-grade climbers, with a range of easy gullies, while the slightly higher and more compact Coire an Lochain has plenty of sterner challenges. Many first ascents have been put up by instructors from nearby Glenmore Lodge, Scotland's National Outdoor Training Centre.

Meall a' Bhuachaille from Cairn Gorm

Loch Garten

Abernethy and Loch Garten

Distance **8.75km/5.5 miles**
Time **2 hours**
Start/Finish **Garten Woods Car Park
(charge) GR NN952190**
Terrain **Woodland and lochside paths**
Map **OS Landranger 36**
Public transport **Regular Stagecoach
Highland Service 34X from Aviemore
and Grantown-on-Spey to Boat of
Garten. This leaves a walk of 1km to
the start**

**Much like Rothiemurchus Forest to
the south, the woodland at
Abernethy is a remnant of the
ancient Caledonian Forest that once
covered a much larger part of
Scotland. Today, Abernethy Forest is
a National Nature Reserve renowned
for its breeding osprey and other
iconic Speyside wildlife. Fantastic
paths and tracks meander their way
through the woodland to reach the
picturesque shores of Lochs Garten
and Mallachie. The walk also visits
the Loch Garten Osprey Centre
where in spring and summer
cameras beam back live images of
the birds at the nest.**

▶ From the small car park at Garten
Woods, a little east of Boat of Garten on
the B970, walk around a barrier to reach
a fork beside an information board. Turn

103

left here onto a path waymarked for the blue Osprey Trail. Follow this excellent path (part of the Speyside Way) as it runs northeast to the right of the B970, undulating gently through pinewoods.

▶ Once past East Croftmore, the path swings right to head east just to the right of a minor road; this is a tranquil spot where the sharp-eared and keen-eyed may be rewarded by the sound or sight of a Scottish crossbill or crested tit, amongst the many other birds that inhabit this woodland.

▶ Walk past a lochan with a viewing bridge to soon arrive at a blue waymark. Turn left to cross the road, continuing in the same direction by a good path on the opposite side. You now leave the Speyside Way behind as it peels off to the left. In time, the path passes the entrance to the Loch Garten car park and carries on for almost another 1km to reach the RSPB's famed osprey-viewing centre where, in spring, early birds (5.30am-8am) can also watch out for the elusive capercaillie.

▶ Once you've checked out the ospreys (usually resident April to August), retrace your steps and walk through the Loch Garten car park to join the green nature trail which heads down to the wooded shores of Loch Garten itself. The path hugs the shore and then bears right to a junction. Turn left onto a wider path and follow this away from the water through ever more scenic forest, the woodland floor carpeted with wildflowers in spring and summer.

▶ Another few hundred metres bring you to the equally alluring Loch Mallachie. Bear right and follow the

Travelling Companions For 60 years the name Loch Garten has been synonymous with the return of breeding osprey to Scotland. It was here, in 1954, that the species first bred, having been persecuted to extinction in Scotland in 1916. Today, the bird's nest site is overlooked by the RSPB's purpose-built Osprey Centre where visitors can learn more about the behaviour of this fish-eating raptor through a combination of telescopes, CCTV images and expert interpretation. A migratory species, ospreys winter in West Africa, usually returning to these shores by late March to breed. Eggs are laid in April and hatch after around 40 days. Within seven weeks the chicks are ready to fly, and by the end of August juveniles and adult birds begin the long journey south for the winter. The Osprey Centre is open daily from April until the end of August (charges apply).

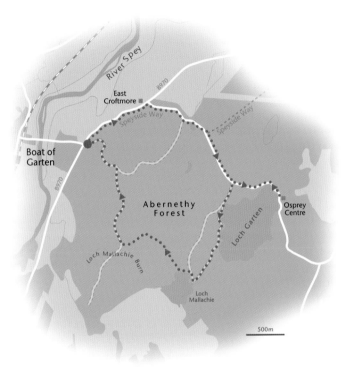

path along the loch's north shore. At its northwestern edge, turn left from the green trail onto a narrower path, which soon veers away from the loch. The woodland here is home to pine marten and capercaillie, although it takes sharp eyes and a lot of luck to spot them. More readily seen are the red squirrels that also make their home here.

▶ Follow the path for just over 1km to a junction, turning right onto a wider track that continues through the trees for a further 1km or so to another junction. Here, turn left onto a track to join the red nature trail and meander through the woodland, eventually dropping gently back downhill to the Garten Woods car park.

Loch Mallachie

Anagach Woods

Grantown -on-Spey and Anagach Woods

Distance 4.5km/2.75 miles
Time 1 hour 15
Start/Finish The Square, Grantown-on-Spey GR NJ035281
Terrain Pavement, single-track road, woodland paths and tracks
Map OS Landranger 36
Public transport Regular Stagecoach Highland Service 34X from Inverness and Aviemore to Grantown-on-Spey

Nestled between handsome Grantown-on-Spey and the river itself, Anagach Woods offer a variety of waymarked walks in picturesque surroundings. This route follows the blue trail and is an ideal length for younger children. The paths are excellent throughout and the walk can easily be extended to include the longer red trail.

► From the war memorial at the heart of Grantown's stately Square, walk southwest towards the High Street, turning left at the end of The Square onto Forest Road. This crosses South Street at the fire station and continues to a small car park at Anagach Woods. Carry on through the car park onto an

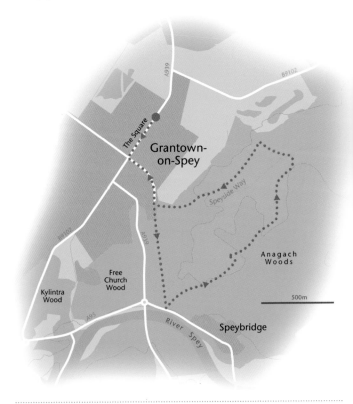

Trees of Life Rather than dark, impenetrable conifer plantations, much of the woodland along the River Spey contains a wildlife-rich mix of native species, with many individual specimens several hundred years old. The community-owned Anagach Woods are no different and the trails here are a joy to explore. The planting of Scots pine, oak and birch began in the 1760s when many trees were transported as saplings from the great Abernethy Forest to the south. Although the majority were lost to timber production, a few of these originals still survive today.

old military road, signposted for woodland trails. Follow the blue waymarkers that lead you through the woodland on a wide track.

► After the last house and a gate, the track splits in three: take the middle one, joining the Speyside Way, and continue south through the wood to an information board after 500m. Here, the track splits again. For a short diversion, go right, cross a minor road and drop down a flight of steps to reach a lovely section of river, close to the Spey Bridge.

► Retrace your steps as far as the information board and turn right to dive back into Anagach Woods, leaving the Speyside Way behind. Bear right at the next fork, with the path soon swinging right and then left, and steeper slopes dropping away on both sides. The meandering path gives great views to the rolling Cromdale Hills, eventually sweeping left at a fork and then dropping down to a junction.

► Turn left here for a gradual descent past several magnificent Scots pines. At the next junction, go straight on; then, shortly after, turn right at a fork. The easy walking continues to another junction: turn left here onto a wider path and then, just before reaching the perimeter of Grantown golf course, bear left to return to the Speyside Way.

► After crossing a couple of burns, you come to a clearing, with the grassy path clinging to its right-hand edge. At a junction, turn right and follow the path as it swings left back into the wood.

► Beyond a gate, cross a small car park and follow its access road past some curling ponds to return to the main car park. Turn right onto Forest Road and retrace your steps to the start.

Granted Lands The handsome town of Grantown-on-Spey was founded in 1766 by local laird Sir James Grant (taking its name from its architect-in-chief). At this time, it developed primarily as a place to rehouse tenants displaced by agricultural reform imposed on Grant lands. Prior to this, the main settlement in the area was on the eastern banks of the Spey at Cromdale, but when the river was bridged to carry a new military road in 1754, the flatter plains to the west seemed a natural site for development. A century later, the arrival of not one but two railway lines helped feed burgeoning industries such as wool, candle making and whisky distilling. More importantly still, the railway brought a steady stream of Victorian tourists – a crucial flow of income that continues today.

River Spey and Anagach Woods

Grantown-on-Spey woodland viewpoints

Distance 5.25km/3.25 miles
Time 1 hour 30
Start/Finish The Square, Grantown-on-Spey GR NJ035281
Terrain Pavement, single-track road, woodland paths and tracks
Map OS Landranger 36
Getting There Regular Stagecoach Highland Service 34X from Inverness and Aviemore to Grantown-on-Spey

Situated just north of the Cairngorm and west of the Cromdale Hills, with woodland all around, Grantown has an enviable location. It also has many fine walks right on its doorstep – this one climbs to the north through woodland to survey the town from not one but three fine viewpoints.

► From the war memorial at the heart of The Square (A939), head southwest towards the High Street, turning right at the end of The Square onto Seafield Avenue. Follow this road as it slips from the bustling town centre, past the leafy gardens of Victorian and Georgian villas, to reach peaceful countryside.

► Just past the entrance to Grantown-on-Spey Caravan Park, the road curves left and soon passes under the Dulicht Bridge. Immediately after the railway arch, turn right to join the Dava Way path (which links Grantown-on-Spey with Forres), signed for the Viewpoints.

► This directs you over a footbridge, through a gate and up some steps onto a dismantled railway line. Go left to follow this for around 100m before turning left off the old railway at a waymarker by a gate. A fenced path then climbs steeply through woodland to reach a viewpoint on the left and another on the right. Both give fine views over Grantown and along the River Spey.

► After the second viewpoint, head through a gate and continue a steady

Way to Go Relatively undiscovered compared to some of Scotland's more established long-distance walks, the Dava Way runs for 38km between Grantown-on-Spey and the historic town of Forres on the Moray Firth. A great off-road cycle as well as a walk, much of the route follows the old Highland Railway Line as it passes through a gentle mix of wood, moor and farmland. The way provides a link between the Speyside Way in the south and the Moray Coastal Trail in the north, so there is plenty of opportunity to extend the adventure if time and energy allow.

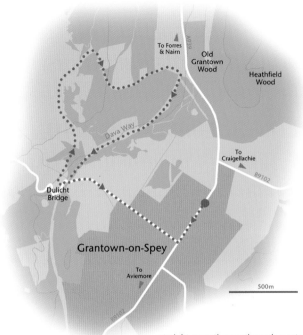

ascent through the woodland, passing several benches along the way. When the path meets a broad track, turn left to gain a final viewpoint, which sits just to the right within a stand of Scots pine.

► Return to the track, turn right and, as it sweeps left, bear right at a waymarker. From here, a path drops down through the pinewood to gain a track. Go

straight on and, once through a gate, follow a rough road as it descends gradually past several cottages.

► Just before the A939, turn right to rejoin the Dava Way (signposted for Grantown-on-Spey) and follow the path as it cuts its way through rocky outcrops, eventually reaching the outbound path after around 0.75km. Retrace your steps off the old railway line, under the bridge and then back along Seafield Avenue to the town centre.

Cromdale Hills from Grantown-on-Spey

Ben Rinnes

Distance 6.5km/4.25 miles
Time 3 hours
Start/Finish Small car park, Glack
Harnes Road GR NJ284360
Terrain Mountain paths and tracks
Map OS Landranger 28
Public transport None to start

Visible for miles around, shapely
Ben Rinnes rises above the flatter
plains of Morayshire, deep in the
heart of whisky country. Good paths
line this walk, although the final
300m to the summit are steep.
However, since the route begins
from a height of around 350m,
Ben Rinnes is the perfect mountain
for a half-day stroll, or for older
children to climb.

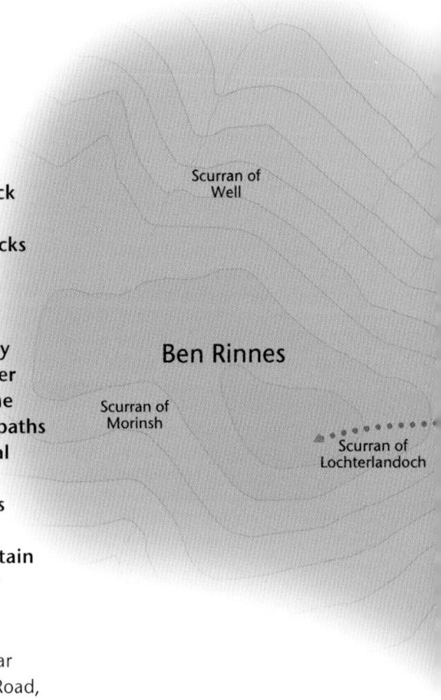

Scurran of Well

Ben Rinnes

Scurran of Morinsh

Scurran of Lochterlandoch

► The walk begins from a small car
park on the narrow Glack Harnes Road,
just a short distance from the B9009
between Dufftown and Glen Livet. Pass
through a gate to join a stony track that
leads up and over Round Hill. The initial
stages are a little eroded, but the path
improves as progress is made.

► Almost immediately, there are fine
views to the nearby peak of Meikle
Conval and along Glen Rinnes. The track
cuts a course up the long east shoulder
of Ben Rinnes, with the mountain's
summit – complete with its distinctive
tor – eventually coming into view.

► The incline soon eases, but only
for a short spell, with another sustained
pull onto Roy's Hill. Once over this,
the terrain flattens again, with views
north to Spey Bay and the Moray Firth.

► Once at Black Banks, the track
narrows to a path, at which point it's
time to dig in for a steep, prolonged pull
up the ridge. The path is excellent and
there are several stepped sections,
making the ascent a little easier.

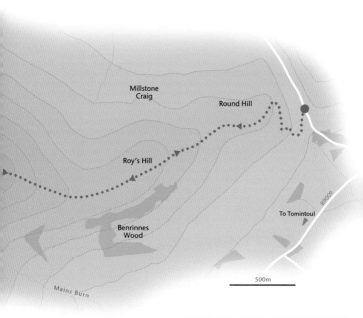

▶ However, Ben Rinnes does not give itself up quite so easily and it is only once you reach the summit at Scurran of Lochterlandoch that the best views are revealed. Look out for ptarmigan huddled on a summit plateau studded with granite tors – which give Ben Rinnes its name 'Hill of the Sharp Point'.

▶ To return to the car park, simply retrace your steps, taking care on the initially steep descent.

High Spirits Ben Rinnes climbs high above the Moray landscape, something of a spiritual home for whisky distilling in Scotland – with several distilleries visible from the summit. On a clear day, you would be hard pushed to find a better viewpoint in this part of Scotland, with the final meanderings of the ever-widening Spey, the Morayshire coast, much of Aberdeenshire and the great expanse of the Cairngorm laid out before you.

Glen Rinnes from Ben Rinnes

Craigellachie Bridge

River Spey at Aberlour

Charlestown of Aberlour and Craigellachie

Distance 7.5km/4.75 miles
Time 2 hours
**Start/Finish High Street, Aberlour
GR NJ266429**
**Terrain Pavement, single-track road,
woodland, riverside paths and tracks**
Map OS Landranger 28
**Public transport Regular Stagecoach
Service 36 from Elgin and Dufftown
to Charlestown of Aberlour**

*Moray is Scotland's malt whisky
country, with Craigellachie and
Charlestown of Aberlour (or just
Aberlour, as it is usually known)
home to three of the many
distilleries that line the Spey here.
This walk links the two villages by
the Speyside Way, visiting an
A-listed Victorian suspension bridge
and returning past Scotland's oldest
surviving wide-span iron bridge
at Craigellachie.*

► Start by the drinking fountain at the
square on the High Street, just opposite
the Co-op. Facing the church, go left to
leave the village centre and pass the
walled Aberlour Old Kirkyard, which
houses the scant remains of St Drostan's
Parish Church.

► At the end of the kirkyard wall,
turn right off the road onto a path
(Aberlour Distillery is just a bit further
on along the road if you fancy a tour).
This path follows the Burn of Aberlour
to reach the Speyside Way. Turn right
onto this to skirt round the bottom of
the kirkyard.

► At a car park, detour left to the
elegant Victoria Bridge which spans the
Spey. Built in 1901 to replace the ferry,
this cast-iron lattice girder footbridge
was known as the Penny Brig after the
toll charged by the Elchies Estate.

Whisky Galore Craigellachie is situated at the confluence of the two rivers most
closely associated with whisky in Scotland: the Spey and the Fiddich. The village
has not one but two distilleries: Craigellachie Distillery, which sits within the
village, and the renowned Macallan Distillery, at its edge by the western banks of
the Spey. The Macallan Distillery was established in 1824 by Alexander Reid, a local
farmer, who obtained one of the first licences to distill whisky legally in Scotland,
while Craigellachie was founded in 1891. The Macallan Distillery can be reached by
way of Craigellachie Bridge – built by Thomas Telford in 1814, with much of the
elaborate latticed metalwork cast in Wales and two mock-medieval towers at either
end. An A-listed structure, it is the oldest wide-span cast-iron bridge in Scotland.

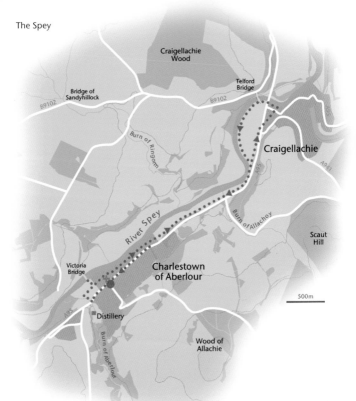

Craigellachie
Wood

Telford
Bridge

Bridge of
Sandyhillock

B9102

B9102

Burn of Ringorm

Craigellachie

A941

River Spey

Burn of Allachoy

Scaut
Hill

Victoria
Bridge

Charlestown
of Aberlour

500m

Distillery

Burn of Aberlour

Wood of
Allachie

► Return across the car park to continue under the arch of a former railway bridge. Just after this, an opening takes you into the riverside park where the Highland Games are held each summer. A path runs parallel to the car park access road, along the old Aberlour railway platform and past the Station House, which is now the Speyside Way Visitor Centre.

► The Speyside Way then continues by the north side of Aberlour Parish Church(set back from the High Street where you started the walk), with views soon opening up along the Spey to the domed summit of Ben Aigan. After a while, it leads you over a minor road and past a small industrial estate as it leaves Aberlour on a lovely wooded section that makes for easy walking.

► After crossing another road and a bridge over a burn, the path's previous life as a railway line is much in evidence – hemmed in by steep embankments, it now heads through a long tunnel.

► Eventually, it swings right to take you under the A95, before passing a football pitch and under a roadbridge. Just after this, turn right up a flight of steps to reach Victoria Street in Craigellachie.

► After exploring the village, return down the steps on Victoria Street but, instead of joining the Speyside Way, go straight across it onto a path which passes along the right edge of a park. Just beyond this, in the right-hand corner of a car park, a path dives under the A941 and through a pocket of woodland to reach a sandy little beach beside the Thomas Telford-designed Craigellachie Bridge.

► With the River Spey at your back, take a path to the right of the outbound path; then, just before you emerge at a small car park, turn right under an old roadbridge to arrive at a rough road. Turn right to follow this as it swings through a gate and back along the river.

► After some fishing huts, the road narrows to a track and carries on by the water. At an embankment, some steps take you up to the outbound section of the Speyside Way, where you turn right to retrace your steps as far as the gate at the end of the small industrial estate.

► Leave the Speyside Way here to turn left up a side road, arriving on the High Street on the edge of Aberlour. It is said that Aberlour's first houses were built from stone dragged from the bed of the Spey, and this route now turns right to follow the pavement past many fine stone properties back to the start.

Loud and Proud The history of Charlestown of Aberlour (or simply Aberlour, as it is known) dates back more than a thousand years to when the missionary St Drostan used water from the nearby burns to baptise local people. Later, the tiny settlement of Skirdustan grew near the confluence of the Lour Burn and the Spey. As the village expanded it eventually took on the name Aberlour which translates beautifully (from a combination of Pictish and Gaelic) as 'The Loud Confluence'. In 1812, the local laird, Charles Grant of Wester Elchies, wanted to develop Aberlour east along the Spey and subsequently decided to put his name to the expanded village – hence Charlestown of Aberlour. Today, Aberlour is home to a distillery – established by James Fleming in 1879 – and Walkers Shortbread, the largest independent biscuit maker in Britain, which produces the bulk of all shortbread exported from Scotland.

Bellie Church, Fochabers

Fochabers and the Spey

Distance **3.5km/2.25 miles**
Time **1 hour**
Start/Finish **The Square, Fochabers
GR NJ345588**
Terrain **Pavement, single-track road,
woodland, riverbank paths**
Map **OS Landranger 28**
Public transport **Regular Stagecoach
Bluebird Service 10 from Elgin to
Fochabers**

This short walk begins from the
centre of Fochabers and winds its
way through woodland to reach the
River Spey at The Intake – where
water from the river was once
channelled into a canal to help drive
a nearby power station.

▶ The Square in the centre of Fochabers
is dominated by the striking Bellie
Church, built by the 4th Duke of Gordon
in 1797. Facing the church, head for
George Street at The Square's right-hand
corner. This takes you away from the
centre and across South Street to reach
the Burn of Fochabers. Turn right and
walk along a riverside path, crossing West
Street to continue and turning left when
you next meet a road (with Fochabers
Memorial Garden to your right).

▶ This takes you over the burn on a
footbridge where, beyond, a narrow

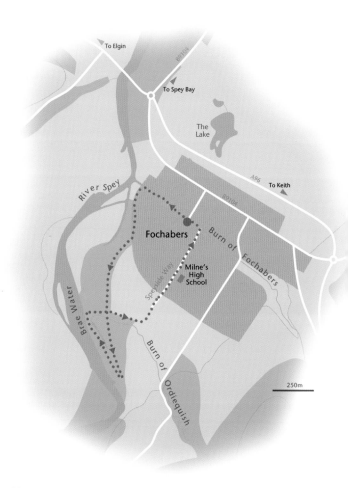

road leads through The Quarters. Take the right branch at a small roundabout and go right again at a T-junction. After this, the road soon narrows to a dirt track. Keep right at a fork and head around a metal barrier onto a fine woodland track. As you walk, look out for short sections of the old canal wall.

▶ When the track forks, head straight on and continue to a crossroads. Again, go straight on, following the path all the way to the Spey at The Intake. This is a peaceful spot, popular with anglers, where the river flows languidly through the landscape.

▶ Turn right down some stone steps onto a woodland path, which wends its way roughly parallel to the Spey. Cross a footbridge and turn right at the next junction to meet the outbound path.

▶ Go straight across this, heading east on a path signposted for Fochabers which leads into another pleasant section of woodland. The path soon bears left to run alongside the little Burn of Ordiequish and then climbs left up wooden steps onto a path known locally as The Sheepie's Roadie. This runs between fields and a strip of woodland, then veers right to a fork.

▶ Go left here along a path which passes to the right of a small housing estate. Beyond a gate, it emerges on Spey Road at a roundabout. Turn right, passing Milne's High School as the road becomes West Street. When this sweeps left, cross back over the Fochabers Burn on a small bridge. Turn left to follow the waterside path back to George Street, heading right to return to The Square.

Home Cooking The attractive village of Fochabers dates from 1776 when it was planned, at the behest of the 4th Duke of Gordon, to replace an older village that he felt had an 'inconvenient nearness' to Gordon Castle – the original seat of the Dukes of Gordon. In 1868, 25-year-old George Baxter, a gardener employed on the Gordon Castle Estate, borrowed money from family members and opened a small grocery shop in the village. He and his wife Margaret began making an assortment of home-made jams and jellies using produce from the local area. Finding favour with the Duke and guests, the enterprise grew into the bestselling Baxters brand, with soup now its most famous product. Fochabers remains the home of Baxters with a large factory and visitor centre.

Anglers on the Spey at Fochabers

Elgin

Distance 4km/2.5 miles
Time 1 hour 15
Start/Finish St Giles Church,
High Street GR NJ215629
Terrain Pavement, parkland paths
Map OS Landranger 28
Public transport Scotrail Services
from Inverness and Aberdeen to
Elgin. Regular Stagecoach Bluebird
Services 10/35A from Inverness and
Aberdeen to Elgin

Sitting to the west of the Spey is
the former cathedral city of Elgin
– a historic town known both for
its handsome architecture and
turbulent past. The River Lossie
cuts through the centre of the town
and this walk makes use of pavement,
parkland and riverside paths to visit
many of Elgin's most historic sites.

▶ Elgin's High Street is dominated
by the magnificent neo-classical
St Giles Church (St Giles is the Patron
Saint of Elgin). From the fountain and
war memorial on the Plainstones at its
front, head round the back of the
church and follow the High Street,
ignoring Commerce Street and Lossie
Wynd intersecting to the right and then
left, to reach a fork at its very end.
Bear left onto North College Street
here, passing the excellent Elgin
Museum housed in an A-listed
Italianate-style building.

Elgin Boating Pond

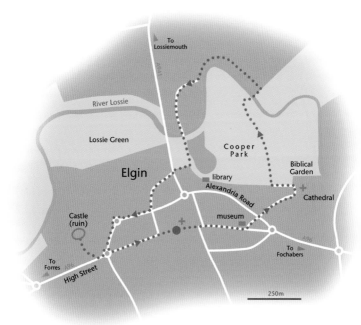

► Cross the main A96 (Alexandra Road) to continue along North College Street, with leafy Cooper Park to your left and the magnificent remains of Elgin Cathedral ahead. Turn left onto King Street to reach the entrance to the cathedral (fee payable to explore the grounds). Just around the corner is the peaceful Biblical Garden, with many plants from the scriptures as well as sculptures depicting scenes from the Bible (open in summer).

► Opposite the cathedral is an entrance to Cooper Park. Pass through the stone gateposts, with the Bishop's House across the grass to your right, and then take the first road on the right (before Cooper Park Bowling Club), following it past the tennis courts and beyond until you reach the banks of the River Lossie.

► Cross the river on Deanshaugh Bridge, turning left onto a paved waterside path that makes its way through an area known as Bishopmill. As the path forks, keep left beside the river before bearing right onto Waterside Street, where you leave the river behind.

▶ At the end of this road, take a left onto Bridge Street (by the Moray Motor Museum). Cross back over the Lossie and bear left into Cooper Park, skirting along the attractive boating pond to your left. On reaching a car park near the water, turn right to head out to the main road (Cumming Street). Cross this onto Trinity Place, where you

Fall and Rise The ancient capital of Moray, Elgin was granted Royal Burgh status by King David I in 1136 and later became a cathedral city when Pope Honorius decreed that the cathedral of Moray should move to its current location just to the east of the city centre on the banks of the Lossie. The notorious Alexander Stewart, better known as the Wolf of Badenoch, burned down the cathedral and much of Elgin in 1390 in revenge for his excommunication, on the grounds of marital infidelity, by the Bishop of Elgin. Both the cathedral and Elgin itself were rebuilt with the city subsequently reinventing itself as a fine location for wealthy Highland landowners to live, as well as a popular tourist destination with the coming of the railway.

pass Elgin's Town Hall, designed by celebrated Scottish architect William Hardie Kininmonth in the 1950s, and, further on to the right, Holy Trinity Church, before swinging right onto Blackfriars Road.

▶ This leads to a supermarket entrance at a roundabout – cross this access road and Haugh Road beyond to continue roughly in the same direction, now on Alexandra Road. At the next roundabout, bear right to shortly reach the entrance to Ladyhill. Turn right through two sets of gateposts and climb a steep flight of steps to the summit – adorned by the huge Duke of Gordon Monument. The column was erected in 1839 in tribute to George Gordon, the 5th Duke of Gordon, who is buried in the grounds of Elgin Cathedral.

▶ Retrace your steps to Alexandra Road and turn left to cross at a designated crossing point to the bottom of the High Street, just to your right. This then leads you east past Thunderton Place, home to Thunderton House – an inn with an illustrious history as a residence for the King when visiting in the 1500s and, much later, a temporary refuge for Bonnie Prince Charlie. After the junction with North Street, the High Street is pedestrianised and it is now a short distance back to St Giles Church.

The Esplanade, Lossiemouth

Seatown, Lossiemouth

Regular favourite walk!

Lossiemouth and the River Lossie

Distance **7.5km/4.75 miles**
Time **2 hours**
Start/Finish **Lossiemouth Marina GR NJ239713**
Terrain **Pavement, beach, coastal and woodland paths**
Map **OS Landranger 28**
Public transport **Regular Stagecoach Bluebird Service 33 from Elgin to Lossiemouth**

An attractive and historic town known for its beaches, Lossiemouth stands at the western extremity of Spey Bay, at the outflow of the River Lossie. This picturesque walk begins from Lossiemouth Marina and crosses a variety of terrain, including dune, beach and coastal grassland in an area renowned for its wildlife.

► Set within the town's harbour walls, Lossiemouth Marina was developed in the 1970s following the decline of the fishing industry – so crucial to many of the towns and villages along the Moray Firth coast. The marina contains more than 100 berths and has done much for the local economy in recent years.

► From the marina, follow Pitgaveny Street south along the quayside, turning

143

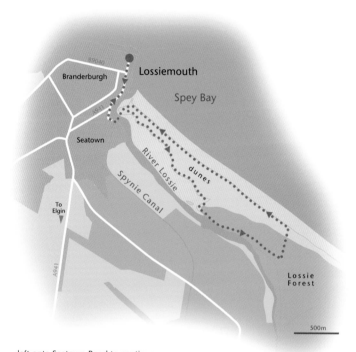

left onto Seatown Road to continue alongside the mouth of the River Lossie and join the esplanade.

► Keep left along the esplanade and then turn left along a side road where the river bends left. This roadway shortly emerges opposite the East Beach car park on Seatown. Go left to cross the Spynie Canal and reach the wooden

footbridge over the clear waters of the River Lossie. As well as being a feature of the walk, this picturesque crossing gives the beach and grassland on the far side a distinctly island feel and you may be torn between lingering above the water or hastening to see what lies on the other side.

▶ With feet planted back on firm land, turn right to walk along the shoreline (or higher up alongside the dunes if the tide is in). As you continue southeast between the dunes and the river, sand soon gives way to coastal grassland. This is an important habitat for many waders and shorebirds – from heron to knot and greenshank – while you may even spot a hunting osprey during the summer.

Hand of Man Lossiemouth's two beaches – East and West – are a delight, although one is not as natural as it seems. The sand dunes along the initial section of East Beach were created artificially in the 1900s by placing disused railway carriages behind the beach, leaving the wind to do the rest. The resulting dunes are a lovely feature, although their creation was designed not for good looks but to provide shelter to the Seatown district and that section of the River Lossie. Another nearby man-made feature is the 10km-long Spynie Canal which flows into the Lossie by its mouth. Built in the early 19th century, its purpose was not one of transport, but instead to drain a low-lying area of land for agricultural use.

▶ Follow the line of the dunes until they eventually sweep right; here, a path leads down to the river and you are forced along a narrow strip of grassland between the river and the dunes. The trail eventually widens and enters the peaceful pine woodland of Lossie Forest.

▶ After a while, the path splits: take the left branch and then, just before a clearing, head left again onto a sandy path. Follow this as it climbs through heather-covered dunes but, just as it sweeps left, leave the path and trees behind to cross the extensive dunes onto stony Lossiemouth Beach. Turn left to bear northwest, soon with soft sand beneath your feet and towering dunes above.

▶ This is a beautiful beach for walking, extending for around 2km back to Lossiemouth, with fine views of the town. Not surprisingly, the crashing breakers are popular with surfers.

▶ Just before you reach the mouth of the river at the far end, look for a gap in the dunes which takes you back to the wooden footbridge. From here, retrace your steps to the marina.

River Lossie

Osprey sculpture at Spey Bay

20/3/18 A great walk on a bright sunny day ☺
A favourite

Kingston and Spey Bay

Distance 7.5km/4.75 miles
Time 2 hours
Start/Finish Kingston GR NJ340655
Terrain Quiet roads, woodland paths
Map OS Landranger 28
Public transport Regular Stagecoach Bluebird Service 34 from Elgin to Kingston

The River Spey reaches the end of its epic journey at Spey Bay, where it flows into the Moray Firth. The estuary is flanked by the village of Kingston on one side and a scattering of houses, along with the excellent Scottish Dolphin Centre, at Spey Bay on the other. This walk uses quiet roads and paths to link both in a wonderfully elemental spot for viewing marine wildlife.

► From the little car park by the waterside at Kingston, make your way through the village, using a narrow path that runs on the left-hand side of Kingston Road. This passes reedbeds and then the Garmouth & Kingston Golf Club to arrive in Garmouth. Here, you follow Spey Street and then Church Street to make the gradual climb through this attractive little village.

► Garmouth has strong links with shipbuilding, although it is perhaps best known as the place where, in 1650, King Charles II landed on his return from exile to sign the Solemn League and Covenant which confirmed the alliance between the English Parliament and Scottish Covenanters in their disputes with the Royalists.

► Pass The Loanie (where the signing took place) and, just before the Garmouth Hotel, turn left onto Church Road. Walk past several houses and, once across a bridge, turn left down some steps, signposted for Spey Bay.

► These take you onto a cycle/walkway, where you turn right to follow this scenic wooded track above the golf course.

Shipping News In 1784, two shipbuilders, William Osborne and Ralph Dodsworth, arrived from Kingston-upon-Hull, having struck a deal with the Duke of Gordon to buy all of the timber in his vast forest at Glenmore. The Spey was already well-used for floating timber from elsewhere for processing at Garmouth, but the two men had even bigger plans. They established shipyards at what was subsequently named Kingston-on-Spey that were capable of building boats of up to 500 tons – including clipper ships that serviced the tea trade from India in the early 1800s. But the boom didn't last long: diminishing timber stocks and the rise to prominence of steel-hulled ships spelt the end of shipbuilding at Kingston-on-Spey.

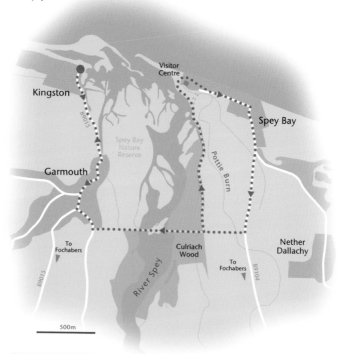

Journey's End Spey Bay is the largest shingle beach system in Scotland – an ever-changing landscape created by the often violent coming together of river and sea. The Spey is unusual in that it actually picks up speed as it reaches the sea, dragging with it vast quantities of shingle. The habitat here ranges from bare shingle to reedbeds and saltmarsh, with a corresponding range of flora and fauna, including osprey, nesting terns at the river mouth and large numbers of wildfowl. Perhaps best of all are the bottlenose dolphins – one of just two such resident populations in British waters – that can often be seen hunting salmon just offshore. You can learn much more about these charismatic animals by visiting the Whale and Dolphin Conservation's Scottish Dolphin Centre, housed in a former salmon fishing station at Spey Bay.

The highlight of this section is the crossing of the historic Spey Viaduct. Opened in 1886, it once carried the Elgin to Buckie section of the Moray Coast Railway over the Spey. Today, it provides a nostalgic means of crossing the by now heavily-braided river as it travels the last few hundred metres to the sea.

► Once across the viaduct, the path continues beyond a car park to a crossroads. Turn left along a track running to the right of Spey Bay woodland (part of a reserve managed by the Scottish Wildlife Trust). Where the track swings right, continue straight on along another track between the Spey and the Pottie Burn.

► At a fork, bear left and follow the line of the river all the way to the shingle beach at Spey Bay, reached via a footbridge and gate. Walk through the car park, passing the historic arches of the Tugnet Ice House − once used to store river ice to preserve salmon caught in nearby waters − and the excellent Scottish Dolphin Centre on your right. A road continues through Spey Bay, with glorious views up and down the coast.

► Follow the road inland when it swings right at the Spey Bay Hotel, the long ridge of Ben Rinnes forming a shapely outline in the distance. Continue along the pavement for around 1km to reach the Moray Railway cycle/walkway, signposted for Garmouth.

► Turn right here and follow the trail between fields to the outbound path at a crossroads. Go straight on to retrace your steps over the viaduct and back to Kingston.

River Spey at Garmouth

Buckie War Memorial

27/12/17 *A bracing walk in sun + blue skies* ☺

Portgordon and Buckie

Distance 7.5km/4.75 miles
Time 2 hours
Start/Finish Portgordon Harbour
GR NJ397643
Terrain Pavement, countryside and coastal paths
Map OS Landranger 28
Public transport Regular Stagecoach Bluebird Service 35 from Inverness and Aberdeen to Portgordon

Located at the east end of Spey Bay, Buckie is the start point for the famous long-distance Speyside Way, which travels for nearly 130km to Aviemore. Rather shorter in length, this simple but scenic walk starts in nearby Portgordon and links the two communities by a coastal stretch of the Speyside Way that is perfect for seal-spotting.

▶ Start at the car park at the east end of Portgordon Harbour. Walk west along the harbourside, turning right at its end onto the High Street (A990) to continue beside the water before swinging inland on Station Road.

▶ Climb steadily past Earls View to reach a path on the left, signposted for Buckie. This cycle/walkway (part of the old Moray Coast Railway Line) leads you northeast between embankments.

▶ After walking down a flight of steps, cross a minor road and carry on along the path (signposted Gollachy Circular) as it runs above the tight street plan of Portgordon. The path leads out of the village and, in time, crosses the Burn of Gollachy to reach a fork. Turn left to head inland (going right would give you a much shorter loop back to Portgordon via the coast), now climbing gradually through gorse to a crossroads.

▶ Go right here to take a path which skirts around Buckpool Golf Course. Emerging on a minor road, turn left and follow this as it winds around the edge of the golf course to join Golf View Drive on the edge of Buckie.

▶ At a junction, cross Barhill Road onto St Peter's Road, aiming for St Peter's Church in the distance ahead. At the

Community Links In 1797, the 4th Duke of Gordon amalgamated the three communities of Port Gordon, Gollachy and Seatown of Tannachy to form Portgordon (the Duke had earlier established the villages of Tomintoul and Fochabers). He contracted ten fishermen and their families to move to the new village and had houses built for them. Another four families moved from Lossiemouth in 1800 and, over the next 60 years, the population grew to almost 700. The current harbour at Portgordon was built in the early 1870s and, at its peak, had a capacity for up to 350 boats, with the main export being corn.

roundabout in front of the church, bear right to curve round onto West Church Street, crossing the Burn of Buckie and continuing all the way to Cluny Square roundabout with its impressive war memorial to the left. This square is the official start of the Speyside Way.

▶ Make a left onto North High Street and, where it sweeps right, exit left onto the A990. Pass the coastguard station, then bear right onto a side street at Yardie – a conservation area and one of the oldest parts of Buckie. This lane leads above the rocky shore, past several houses and drying greens. Where it rejoins the A990, turn right for a brief section on the main road.

▶ Shortly after crossing the Burn of Buckie, join the Speyside Way (also the Moray Coast Trail) just to the right of the A990. Turn right onto a side road after only 70m before almost immediately leaving this for another path on the right. The parkland you are now passing through was once part of Buckpool Old Harbour, filled in during the 1970s, though the harbour walls still remain.

▶ At the end of this path, a small lane leads you on along the seaward side of town, the gable ends of the houses turned to the sea for protection. Beyond two white posts, a path takes over once more, with views over the Moray Firth to

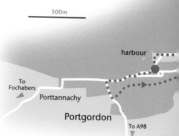

the distant Caithness hills. Again, you have to return briefly 'inland' onto the A990, passing the front of a row of terraced houses, but you can return to the seaward side of Buckpool's houses on a grassy track just beyond.

▶ This takes you above the shore and out of Buckie, and soon becomes a stony track. Not long after passing a derelict cottage, the track emerges on the A990 by a house for another short section of pavement; cross the Burn of Gollachy before returning to the coastal path to pass a favourite haul-out site for both grey and common seals.

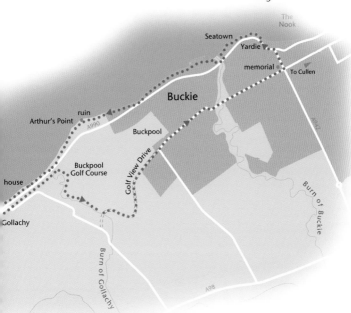

▶ Approaching Portgordon, the route passes an early 19th-century turf-roofed ice house, unusual for its exposed position so close to the shore. With the rocky coastline now giving way to shingle beach, the track soon joins a narrow road which takes you past the end of Shore Street and then Cathcart Street. When the road you're on swings left, bear right onto a rougher lane and follow this as it curves round to Portgordon Harbour and the start.

Harbour Town Straddling the mouth of the Burn of Buckie, the town of Buckie was formed by the coming together of several fishing villages: Easter Buckie, Nether Buckie (now Buckpool), Yardie, Ianstown, Gordonsburgh and Portessie.

A new town was laid out in the early 1800s on a ridge behind the fishing villages by the local lairds, the Gordons of Cluny. Later, in 1877, the same family built the impressive harbour that remains the beating heart of Buckie today. Although not as busy as it once was, this is as good a place as any in Scotland to watch a fishing fleet go about its daily business.

Portgordon from Buckie

Index